HURRY-UP
CHICKEN
RECIPES

PUBLICATIONS INTERNATIONAL, LTD.

ISBN: 1-56173-405-5

Cover photography and photography on pages 7, 35, 41, 49 and 77 by
Ray Reiss Photography, Chicago
Photo Stylist: Laura 't Hart
Food Stylist: Becky Roller

Manufactured in U.S.A.

8 7 6 5 4 3 2 1

Pictured on the front cover (*clockwise from bottom left*): Mexican-Style Almond Chicken Salad (*page 21*), Double-Coated Chicken (*page 67*) and Chicken Macadamia (*page 79*).

Pictured on the back cover (*clockwise from top left*): Orange Chicken Oriental (*page 40*), Chicken Luncheon Sandwich (*page 6*), Hearty Chicken and Rice Soup (*page 22*) and Chicken Picante (*page 54*).

Microwave ovens vary in wattage and power output; cooking times given with microwave directions in this book may need to be adjusted.

101+
HURRY-UP
CHICKEN
RECIPES

Deluxe Fajita Nachos

2½ cups shredded cooked chicken
1 package (1.27 ounces) LAWRY'S®
    Spices & Seasonings for Fajitas
⅓ cup water
8 ounces tortilla chips
1¼ cups (5 ounces) grated
    Cheddar cheese
1 cup (4 ounces) grated Monterey
    Jack cheese
1 large tomato, chopped
1 can (2¼ ounces) sliced ripe
    olives, drained
¼ cup sliced green onions
    Salsa

In medium skillet, combine chicken,
Spices & Seasonings for Fajitas and
water; blend well. Bring to a boil;
reduce heat and simmer 3 minutes.
In large shallow ovenproof platter,
arrange chips. Top with chicken and
cheeses. Place under broiler to melt
cheese. Top with tomato, olives,
green onions and desired amount
of salsa.

*Makes 4 appetizer or
2 main-dish servings*

Presentation: Garnish with guacamole
and sour cream.

Hint: For a spicier version, add sliced
jalapeños.

New Yorker Pita Sandwich

¾ pound boneless skinless
    chicken breasts, cut into
    ¼-inch strips
½ cup chopped onion
½ cup green bell pepper strips
1 tablespoon vegetable oil
1 can (16 ounces) HEINZ
    Vegetarian Beans in Tomato
    Sauce
2 tablespoons HEINZ Horseradish
    Sauce
¼ teaspoon salt
    Dash black pepper
4 pocket pita breads (5-inch
    diameter)
8 slices tomato
    Leaf lettuce

In skillet, sauté chicken, onion and
green pepper in oil until vegetables
are tender-crisp and chicken is
tender. Stir in beans, horseradish
sauce, salt and pepper. Simmer
5 minutes to blend flavors. Cut pitas
in half and tuck 1 tomato slice and
lettuce into each half. Fill each with
about ⅓ cup bean mixture.

*Makes 4 servings
(about 3 cups mixture)*

Deluxe Fajita Nachos

4

Barbecued Chicken on a Bun

- 1 teaspoon seasoned salt
- ⅛ teaspoon coarsely ground black pepper
- 2 whole boneless chicken breasts, halved
- 4 buns, split and toasted
- 4 slices (1 ounce *each*) Swiss cheese
- 4 slices (1 ounce *each*) baked ham, warmed
  Peach-Mint Salsa (recipe follows)
  Lettuce leaves
  Savory Grilled Peaches (recipe follows)

Combine seasoned salt and pepper. Loosen one edge of chicken skin and rub seasoning mixture underneath skin. Cook chicken skin-side down on covered grill over medium, indirect heat about 30 to 35 minutes or until chicken is tender and no longer pink. Remove and discard skin. Serve chicken on buns topped with cheese, ham and salsa. Garnish with lettuce. Serve with Savory Grilled Peaches.

Makes 4 hearty sandwiches

Conventional Oven Method: Prepare as above. Roast skin-side up in 350°F oven for about 30 minutes or until chicken is tender and no longer pink. Continue as directed.

Tip: Sandwiches are delicious served either hot or cold.

Peach-Mint Salsa

- 1 fresh California peach, chopped (about ⅔ cup)
- ⅓ cup chopped green onions
- 1 tomato, chopped
- 1½ tablespoons chopped fresh mint
- ¼ teaspoon chili powder

In small bowl, combine all ingredients. Refrigerate leftovers.

Makes about 1½ cups

Savory Grilled Peaches:

Cut 4 fresh California peaches in half. Cook on covered grill over medium, indirect heat 4 minutes. Turn and cook an additional 4 minutes or until heated through.

Makes 4 servings

Favorite recipe from **California Tree Fruit Agreement**

Chicken Luncheon Sandwich

- 1½ cups chopped cooked chicken
- 1 cup (4 ounces) shredded Wisconsin Cheddar cheese
- ½ cup finely chopped celery
- ¼ cup green bell pepper
- 1 green onion, chopped
- 1 tablespoon chopped pimiento
- ½ cup mayonnaise
- ½ cup plain yogurt
  Salt and pepper to taste
  Rolls or bread
  Lettuce leaves

Combine chicken, cheese, celery, bell pepper, onion, pimiento, mayonnaise and yogurt. Season with salt and pepper. Stir until well blended. Refrigerate until ready to use. Serve on rolls with lettuce.

Makes about 4½ cups

Favorite recipe from **Wisconsin Milk Marketing Board © 1992**

Chicken Luncheon Sandwich

Party Chicken Sandwiches

Prep time: 15 minutes
Broiling time: 5 minutes

1½ cups finely chopped cooked
   chicken
1 cup MIRACLE WHIP® Salad
   Dressing
1 4-oz. can chopped green
   chilies, drained
¾ cup (3 ozs.) 100% Natural KRAFT®
   Shredded Sharp Cheddar
   Cheese
¼ cup finely chopped onion
36 party rye or pumpernickel
   bread slices

Combine chicken, salad dressing,
chilies, cheese and onions; mix
lightly. Cover bread with chicken
mixture. Broil 5 minutes or until lightly
browned. Serve hot. Garnish as
desired.   *Makes 3 dozen*

Variation: Substitute MIRACLE WHIP®
Light Reduced Calorie Salad
Dressing for Regular Salad Dressing.

Zesty Liver Pâté

⅓ cup butter or margarine
1 pound chicken livers
¾ cup coarsely chopped scallions
¾ cup chopped parsley
½ cup dry white wine
¾ teaspoon TABASCO® Pepper
   Sauce
½ teaspoon salt
   Crackers or French bread

In large saucepan melt butter; add
chicken livers, scallions and parsley
and sauté until livers are evenly
browned. Transfer to container of
food processor or blender. Add
wine, Tabasco® sauce and salt;
cover. Process until smooth. Pour into
decorative crock-style jar with lid.
Chill until thick enough to spread.
Serve with crackers or French bread.
                    Makes about 2 cups

Southwest Chicken Fingers

⅔ cup HELLMANN'S® or BEST
   FOODS® Real, Light or
   Cholesterol Free Reduced
   Calorie Mayonnaise
⅓ cup prepared salsa
1½ pounds boneless skinless
   chicken breasts, cut into
   3×1-inch strips

In large bowl combine mayonnaise
and salsa; set aside 6 tablespoons.
Add chicken strips to mayonnaise
mixture in large bowl; toss well. Let
stand 30 minutes. Grill chicken
5 inches from heat, turning once,
4 minutes or until chicken is tender.
Or, broil, without turning, 5 inches
from heat. Serve with reserved
sauce.

Makes 6 to 8 appetizer servings

Chicken Swiss-wiches

1½ cups chopped cooked chicken
⅓ cup mayonnaise
¼ cup diced celery
¼ cup diced Wisconsin Swiss
   cheese
8 slices bread
1 can (14½ ounces) asparagus
   spears, drained
½ cup butter
1 package (2⅜ ounces) seasoned
   coating mix for chicken

Combine chicken, mayonnaise,
celery and Swiss cheese. Spread
on 4 slices of the bread. Arrange
asparagus spears on top of filling;
top with remaining bread.

Melt butter on griddle or in skillet;
use to brush outside of sandwiches.
Coat sandwiches with coating mix
for chicken. Grill until center is hot
and coating is golden.

Makes 4 servings

Favorite recipe from **Wisconsin Milk
Marketing Board** © 1992

Party Chicken Sandwiches

Curried Chicken Puffs

½ cup water
⅓ cup PARKAY® Margarine
⅔ cup flour
  Dash of salt
2 eggs
1 8-oz. pkg. PHILADELPHIA BRAND®
  Cream Cheese, softened
¼ cup milk
¼ teaspoon salt
  Dash of curry powder
  Dash of pepper
1½ cups chopped cooked chicken
⅓ cup slivered almonds, toasted
2 tablespoons green onion slices

• Bring water and margarine to boil. Add flour and dash salt; stir vigorously over low heat until mixture forms ball. Remove from heat; add eggs, one at a time, beating until smooth after each addition.

• Place level measuring tablespoonfuls of batter on ungreased cookie sheet.

• Bake at 400°F, 25 minutes. Cool.

• Combine cream cheese, milk, ¼ teaspoon salt, curry powder and pepper, mixing until well blended. Add chicken, almonds and onions; mix lightly.

• Cut tops from cream puffs; fill with chicken mixture. Replace tops. Place puffs on cookie sheet.

• Bake at 375°F, 5 minutes or until warm.
Makes approximately 1½ dozen

Note: Unfilled cream puffs can be prepared several weeks in advance and frozen. Place puffs on a jelly roll pan and wrap securely in moisture-vaporproof wrap.

Muffin Divan

Prep time: 20 minutes
Cooking time: 15 minutes

2 cups chopped cooked chicken
1 cup mushroom slices
⅓ cup picante sauce
¼ cup MIRACLE WHIP® Salad
  Dressing
2 tablespoons green onion slices
3 English muffins, split, toasted
1 cup chopped cooked broccoli
½ lb. VELVEETA® Pasteurized
  Process Cheese Spread,
  sliced

Preheat oven to 350°F. Combine chicken, mushrooms, sauce, salad dressing and onions; mix lightly. Top muffin halves with chicken mixture and broccoli. Place on ungreased cookie sheet. Bake for 10 minutes. Top with process cheese spread; continue baking until process cheese spread begins to melt.
Makes 6 sandwiches

Cajun Chicken Burgers

1 pound fresh ground chicken
1 small onion, finely chopped
¼ cup chopped green or red
  bell pepper
3 scallions, minced
1 clove garlic, minced
1 teaspoon Worcestershire sauce
½ teaspoon TABASCO® Pepper
  Sauce
  Ground black pepper

In medium bowl, combine chicken, onion, bell pepper, scallions, garlic, Worcestershire sauce, Tabasco® sauce and black pepper. Form into five 3-inch patties. Broil or grill 6 minutes; turn over and broil an additional 4 to 6 minutes or until no longer pink. Serve immediately.
Makes 5 servings

Hot Chicken and Pepper Pita

1½ tablespoons vegetable oil
2 whole boneless skinless chicken breasts, cut into cubes
½ teaspoon garlic salt
1 medium-size onion, sliced into thin rings
1 medium-size red bell pepper, cut into strips
1 medium-size yellow bell pepper, cut into strips
1 medium-size green bell pepper, cut into strips
2 teaspoons finely chopped pickled hot pepper rings, drained well (optional)
1 package (12 ounces) OCEAN SPRAY® Cran-Fruit™ Sauce, any flavor
2 tablespoons soy sauce
½ teaspoon ground ginger
⅓ cup cashews
2 cups shredded lettuce
4 large pita breads, halved

Heat oil in skillet at medium heat 2 to 3 minutes. Add chicken; cook and stir until lightly browned. Sprinkle with garlic salt. Add onion and peppers; cook and stir 3 minutes. Stir in Cran-Fruit™ Sauce, soy sauce and ginger. Reduce heat to medium; cook uncovered 5 to 8 minutes until vegetables are crisp tender. Remove from heat; toss lightly with cashews and lettuce. Spoon into pita breads.

Makes 8 sandwiches

Glazed Ginger Chicken

5 tablespoons KIKKOMAN® Soy Sauce
3 tablespoons plum jam
1 tablespoon sesame seed, toasted
1 tablespoon cornstarch
1 tablespoon minced fresh ginger
1 clove garlic, pressed
8 small chicken thighs (about 2 pounds)

Cut eight 8-inch squares of aluminum foil; set aside. Combine soy sauce, plum jam, sesame seed, cornstarch, ginger and garlic in small saucepan. Bring to boil over medium heat, stirring constantly. Remove from heat and cool slightly. Stir in thighs, a few at a time, to coat each piece well. Place 1 thigh, skin-side up, on each foil square. Divide and spoon remaining sauce evenly over thighs. Fold ends of foil to form a package; crease and fold down to secure well. Place foil bundles, seam-side up, in single layer, on steamer rack. Set rack in large pot or wok of boiling water. (Do not allow water level to reach bundles.) Cover and steam 30 minutes or until chicken is tender. Garnish as desired. Serve immediately.

Makes 8 appetizer servings

Mexican Appetizer Cheesecake

3 (8-ounce) packages cream cheese, softened
2 teaspoons WYLER'S® or STEERO® Chicken-Flavor Instant Bouillon
1½ teaspoons chili powder
½ teaspoon hot pepper sauce
2 eggs
½ cup *hot* water
1 cup finely chopped cooked chicken
1 (4-ounce) can chopped green chilies, well drained
Salsa, shredded cheese and sliced green onions
LA FAMOUS® Tortilla Chips

Preheat oven to 325°F. In large mixer bowl, beat cream cheese, bouillon, chili powder and hot pepper sauce until smooth. Add eggs and water; mix well. Stir in chicken and chilies. Pour into 9-inch springform pan. Bake 30 minutes or until set; cool 15 minutes. Carefully run knife around edge of pan; remove side of pan. Top with salsa, cheese and green onions. Serve warm or chilled with tortilla chips. Refrigerate leftovers.

Makes 10 to 12 appetizer servings

Chicken Kabobs in Pita Bread

¼ cup olive or vegetable oil
¼ cup lemon juice
½ teaspoon salt
½ teaspoon dried oregano leaves
¼ teaspoon garlic powder
⅛ teaspoon pepper
1 whole boneless skinless chicken breast, cut into 1-inch cubes
2 large pita breads
1 small onion, thinly sliced
1 tomato, thinly sliced
½ cup plain yogurt
  Parsley, if desired

1. Mix oil, lemon juice, salt, oregano, garlic powder and pepper in medium glass bowl. Add chicken; toss to coat completely. Cover and refrigerate at least 3 hours or overnight.

2. Remove chicken from marinade, reserving marinade. Thread chicken onto 4 small metal skewers. Place kabobs on greased broiler pan. Broil about 5 inches from heat until chicken is golden, 8 to 10 minutes, brushing often with marinade. Turn kabobs over and brush with marinade. Broil until chicken is tender and no longer pink, 5 to 7 minutes.

3. Cut each pita bread in half; gently pull each half open to form a pocket. Remove chicken from 1 kabob and place inside 1 pocket; repeat with remaining kabobs. Top with onion, tomato and yogurt. Garnish with parsley. Serve hot.

Makes 4 servings

Bandito Buffalo Wings

Preparation time: 15 minutes
Total time: 55 minutes

1 package ORTEGA® Taco Seasoning Mix
12 chicken wings, split with tips removed (about 2 pounds)
½ cup ORTEGA® Thick and Chunky Salsa, Green Chile Salsa or Picante Sauce

Place seasoning mix in heavy plastic food storage bag. Add a few chicken wings; shake until well coated. Repeat to coat all pieces. Place in lightly greased baking pan. Bake at 375°F for 35 to 40 minutes or until chicken is tender and juices run clear. Serve hot with salsa for dipping.

Makes 2 dozen appetizers

Microwave Directions: Prepare chicken as above. Place 8 pieces on 9-inch microwaveable pie plate with meaty portions toward edge of plate. Cook at MEDIUM-HIGH (70% power) for 8 to 10 minutes or until chicken is no longer pink near bone, turning dish after 4 minutes. (Chicken should reach an internal temperature of 180°F.) Repeat with remaining pieces. Serve as above.

Grecian Chicken Salad Sandwiches

2 cups chopped cooked chicken
1 cup seeded chopped cucumber
1 cup seeded chopped tomato
⅓ cup sliced green onions
¼ cup REALEMON® Lemon Juice from Concentrate
¼ cup vegetable oil
1 teaspoon sugar
½ teaspoon salt
¼ teaspoon dried basil leaves
1 clove garlic, finely chopped
2 cups shredded lettuce
4 pita bread rounds, halved

In medium bowl, combine chicken, cucumber, tomato and onions. In jar or cruet, combine ReaLemon® brand, oil, sugar, salt, basil and garlic; shake well. Pour over chicken mixture. Cover; marinate in refrigerator 2 hours. Just before serving, toss with lettuce. Serve in pita bread. Refrigerate leftovers.

Makes 4 sandwiches

Chicken Kabobs in Pita Bread

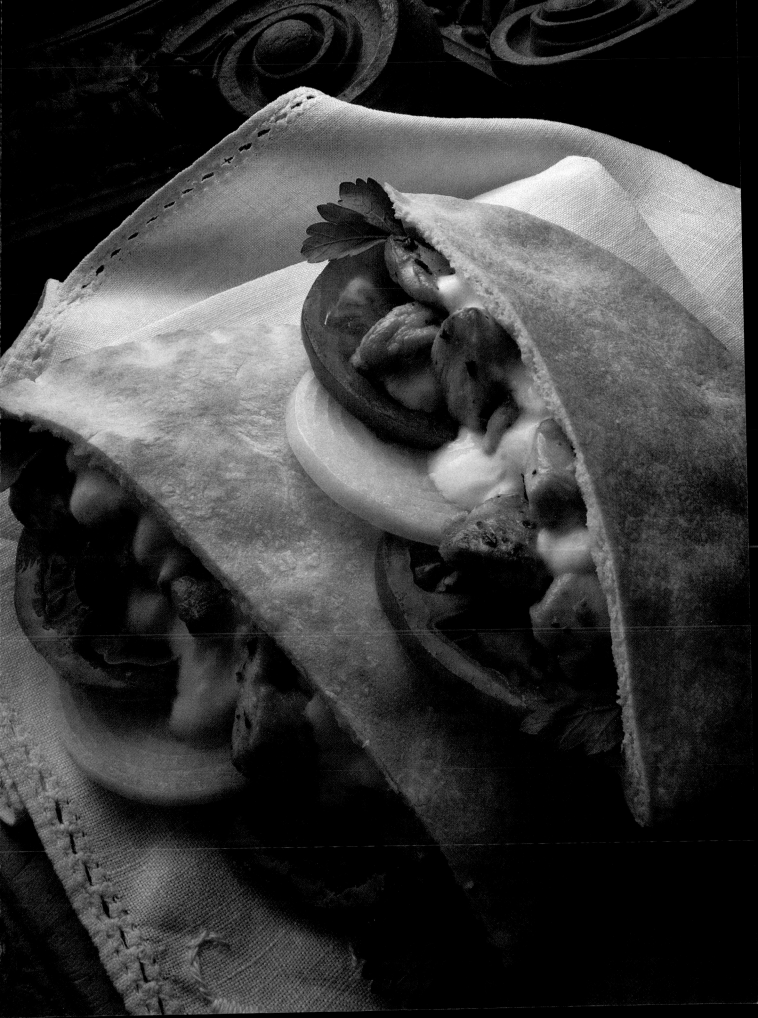

Garlicky Gilroy Chicken Wings

2 pounds chicken wings (about 15 wings)
3 heads fresh garlic,* separated into cloves and peeled
1 cup plus 1 tablespoon olive oil, divided
10 to 15 drops TABASCO® Pepper Sauce
1 cup grated Parmesan cheese
1 cup Italian-style bread crumbs
1 teaspoon black pepper

Preheat oven to 375°F. Disjoint chicken wings, removing tips. (If desired, save tips to make chicken stock.) Rinse wings; pat dry. Place garlic, 1 cup oil and pepper sauce in food processor or blender container; cover and process until smooth. Pour garlic mixture into small bowl. Combine cheese, bread crumbs and black pepper in shallow dish. Dip wings into garlic mixture, then roll, one at a time, in crumb mixture until thoroughly coated. Brush shallow nonstick pan with remaining 1 tablespoon oil; arrange wings in a single layer. Drizzle remaining garlic mixture over wings; sprinkle with remaining crumb mixture. Bake 45 to 60 minutes or until brown and crisp. Garnish as desired.

Makes about 6 appetizer servings

*The whole garlic bulb is called a *head*.

Favorite recipe from **The Fresh Garlic Association**

Bits o' Teriyaki Chicken

½ cup KIKKOMAN® Teriyaki Sauce
1 teaspoon sugar
2 whole boneless skinless chicken breasts, cut into 1-inch pieces
1 tablespoon water
1 teaspoon cornstarch
1 tablespoon vegetable oil
2 tablespoons sesame seed, toasted

Combine teriyaki sauce and sugar in small bowl. Stir in chicken; marinate 30 minutes, stirring occasionally. Remove chicken; reserve 2 tablespoons marinade. Combine reserved marinade, water and cornstarch in small bowl; set aside. Heat oil in hot wok or skillet over medium-high heat. Add chicken and sesame seed; stir-fry 2 minutes. Stir in cornstarch mixture. Cook and stir until mixture boils and thickens and chicken is tender, about 1 minute. Turn into chafing dish or onto serving platter. Serve warm with wooden picks.

Makes 6 appetizer servings

Cheddary Chicken Salad Grills

Prep time: 15 minutes
Cooking time: 10 minutes

2 cups chopped cooked chicken
¼ lb. VELVEETA® Pasteurized Process Cheese Spread, cubed
¼ cup chopped celery
¼ cup KRAFT® Real Mayonnaise
12 whole-wheat bread slices
KRAFT® Strawberry Preserves
Soft PARKAY® Margarine

Combine chicken, process cheese spread, celery and mayonnaise; mix lightly. For each sandwich, spread one bread slice with preserves; cover with chicken mixture and second bread slice. Spread sandwich with margarine. Grill until lightly browned on both sides.

Makes 6 sandwiches

Garlicky Gilroy Chicken Wings

Thai Chicken Strips

½ cup WISH-BONE® Italian Dressing
¼ cup dry white wine
1 tablespoon sugar
1 tablespoon soy sauce
1 tablespoon finely chopped cilantro or parsley
½ teaspoon ground ginger
½ teaspoon ground cumin
¼ teaspoon paprika
¼ cup sesame seeds, well toasted
1½ pounds boneless chicken breasts, cut into lengthwise strips

In food processor or blender, process Italian dressing, wine, sugar, soy sauce, cilantro, ginger, cumin and paprika until blended. In large shallow baking dish, combine dressing mixture, sesame seeds and chicken. Cover and marinate in refrigerator, stirring occasionally, at least 3 hours.

Remove chicken and marinade to large shallow baking pan or aluminum foil-lined broiler rack. Broil chicken with marinade, turning occasionally, 10 minutes or until chicken is tender. Garnish as desired.

Makes about 20 appetizers

Note: Also terrific with WISH-BONE® Robusto Italian, Classic Dijon Vinaigrette, Herbal Italian, Lite Italian, Blended Italian or Lite Classic Dijon Vinaigrette Dressing.

Monte Cristo Sandwiches

⅓ cup HELLMANN'S® or BEST FOODS® Real, Light or Cholesterol Free Reduced Calorie Mayonnaise
¼ teaspoon nutmeg
⅛ teaspoon freshly ground pepper
12 slices white bread, crusts removed
6 slices Swiss cheese
6 slices cooked ham
6 slices cooked chicken
2 eggs
½ cup milk

In small bowl combine mayonnaise, nutmeg and pepper; spread on 1 side of each bread slice. Arrange cheese, ham and chicken on mayonnaise sides of 6 bread slices; top with remaining bread, mayonnaise-sides down. Cut sandwiches diagonally into quarters. In small bowl beat together eggs and milk; dip sandwich quarters into egg mixture. Cook on preheated greased griddle or in skillet, turning once, 4 to 5 minutes or until browned and heated through.

Makes 24 mini sandwiches

Cheesy Chicken Sandwiches

2 tablespoons butter or margarine
¼ cup chopped onion
2 tablespoons flour
1½ cups milk
½ cup shredded Swiss cheese
¼ cup grated Parmesan cheese
½ teaspoon TABASCO® Pepper Sauce
Pinch ground nutmeg
8 slices white bread, toasted, divided
¾ pound sliced cooked chicken
8 slices cooked bacon, divided

Preheat broiler. In small saucepan melt butter; add onion and cook 3 minutes or until golden. Stir in flour; cook 1 minute. Remove from heat. Gradually add milk. Stir constantly; bring to a boil over medium heat and boil 1 minute. Add cheeses, Tabasco® sauce and nutmeg; stir until cheeses are melted. Remove from heat. Place 4 slices toast in shallow baking dish. Arrange chicken on toast; top each sandwich with 1 slice bacon. Spoon sauce over all. Heat under broiler until bubbly and brown. Top with remaining bacon and toast.

Makes 4 servings

Tropical Popovers

¼ cup plain yogurt
¼ cup mayonnaise
1 tablespoon fresh lime or
    lemon juice
1 teaspoon curry powder
2 cups cubed cooked chicken
1¼ cups cubed papaya
½ cup sliced celery
¼ cup chopped green onions
¼ teaspoon salt
    Popovers (recipe follows)
⅓ cup shredded coconut, toasted

Combine yogurt, mayonnaise, lime juice and curry powder in large bowl; mix well. Add chicken, papaya, celery, onions and salt; mix lightly. Chill at least 2 hours or overnight. Prepare Popovers. Place 1 split hot popover on each plate; fill with chicken mixture. Sprinkle with coconut. *Makes 6 servings*

Popovers

2 eggs
1 cup milk
1 cup all-purpose flour
¼ teaspoon salt

Preheat oven to 425°F. Beat eggs with milk in small bowl. Add flour and salt; beat until smooth. Pour equal amounts of batter into six greased custard cups. Place on baking sheet. Bake 40 minutes.
Makes 6 popovers

Note: Popovers may be frozen and reheated.

Stuffed Mushroom Crowns

2 cans (6 ounces each)
    cooked-in-butter mushroom
    crowns*
1 package (3 ounces) cream
    cheese, softened
⅔ cup finely chopped cooked
    chicken
2 teaspoons lemon juice
½ teaspoon onion juice
⅛ teaspoon salt
    Pinch pepper
    Pinch garlic powder
    Paprika

1. Drain mushrooms; reserve crowns. Remove and finely chop stems.

2. Combine cream cheese, mushroom stems, chicken, lemon and onion juices, salt, pepper and garlic powder in small bowl. Spoon mixture into hollow of each mushroom crown. Refrigerate 30 minutes. Sprinkle each crown with paprika.
Makes about 50 appetizers

*If desired, 1 pound small fresh mushrooms can be substituted for the 2 cans cooked-in-butter mushrooms. Remove and finely chop stems. Cook mushroom crowns and chopped stems in 1 to 2 tablespoons butter in skillet just until brown on rounded sides, no more than 3 minutes. Proceed as directed above.

Chicken Wings with Honey & Orange Sauce

12 chicken wings (about 2 pounds)
1 envelope LIPTON® Golden Onion
    Recipe Soup Mix
⅓ cup honey
¼ cup water
¼ cup frozen concentrated
    orange juice, partially thawed
    and undiluted
¼ cup sherry
1 tablespoon prepared mustard
2 teaspoons soy sauce
¼ teaspoon ground ginger
3 dashes hot pepper sauce

Preheat oven to 350°F. Cut tips off chicken wings (save tips for soup, if desired). Halve remaining chicken wings at joint.

In 13×9-inch baking dish, blend remaining ingredients; add chicken and turn to coat. Bake uncovered, basting occasionally, 40 minutes or until chicken is tender and sauce is thickened.
Makes 24 appetizers

Microwave Directions: In 13×9-inch baking dish, prepare chicken wings and sauce as above. Microwave uncovered, at HIGH (Full Power), basting and rearranging chicken occasionally, 20 minutes or until chicken is tender and sauce is thickened. Let stand uncovered 5 minutes.

Fresh Fruity Chicken Salad

Yogurt Dressing (recipe follows)
2 cups cubed cooked chicken
1 cup cantaloupe melon balls
1 cup honeydew melon cubes
½ cup chopped celery
⅓ cup cashews
¼ cup green onion slices
Lettuce leaves

Prepare Yogurt Dressing; set aside. Combine chicken, melons, celery, cashews and green onions in large bowl. Add dressing; mix lightly. Cover. Chill 1 hour. Serve on bed of lettuce. **Makes 4 servings**

Yogurt Dressing

¼ cup plain yogurt
3 tablespoons mayonnaise
3 tablespoons fresh lime juice
¾ teaspoon ground coriander
½ teaspoon salt
Dash of pepper

Combine ingredients in small bowl; mix well. **Makes about ½ cup**

Chicken Noodle Soup

5 (14½-ounce) cans ready-to-serve chicken broth
2 cups water
1 small onion, cut into small wedges
1 cup sliced carrots
1 cup sliced celery (including leaves)
2 tablespoons WYLER'S® or STEERO® Chicken-Flavor Instant Bouillon
1 teaspoon parsley flakes
1 teaspoon basil leaves
¼ teaspoon pepper
½ (1-pound) package CREAMETTE® Egg Noodles, uncooked
2 cups chopped cooked chicken

In Dutch oven, combine broth, water, onion, carrots, celery, bouillon, parsley, basil and pepper. Bring to boil. Reduce heat; simmer 15 minutes. Prepare noodles according to package directions; drain. Add egg noodles and chicken to soup; heat through. Garnish as desired. Refrigerate leftovers. **Makes about 4 quarts**

Fresh Fruity Chicken Salad

Chicken Potato Salad Olé

2 large ripe tomatoes, seeded
    and chopped
¾ cup chopped green onions
¼ cup chopped fresh cilantro
1 to 2 tablespoons chopped,
    seeded, pickled jalapeño
    peppers
1½ teaspoons salt, divided
1 cup HELLMANN'S® or BEST
    FOODS® Real, Light or
    Cholesterol Free Reduced
    Calorie Mayonnaise
3 tablespoons lime juice
1 teaspoon chili powder
1 teaspoon ground cumin
2 pounds small red potatoes,
    cooked and sliced ¼ inch
    thick
2 cups shredded cooked chicken
1 large yellow or red bell pepper,
    diced
    Lettuce leaves
    Tortilla chips, lime slices, whole
    chili peppers and cilantro
    sprigs for garnish (optional)

In medium bowl combine tomatoes,
green onions, chopped cilantro,
jalapeño peppers and 1 teaspoon
of the salt; set aside. In large bowl
combine mayonnaise, lime juice,
chili powder, cumin and remaining
½ teaspoon salt. Add potatoes,
chicken, bell pepper and half of the
tomato mixture; toss to coat well.
Cover; chill. To serve, spoon salad
onto lettuce-lined platter. Spoon
remaining tomato mixture over
salad. If desired, garnish with tortilla
chips, lime slices, whole chili
peppers and cilantro sprigs.

Makes 6 servings

Mexican-Style Almond Chicken Salad

4 boneless skinless chicken breast
    halves, poached
1 cup BLUE DIAMOND® Blanched
    Slivered Almonds
⅓ cup plus 2 teaspoons vegetable
    oil, divided
6 tablespoons lime juice
3 cloves garlic, finely chopped
5 teaspoons ground cumin
⅛ teaspoon cayenne pepper
½ teaspoon salt
6 tablespoons mayonnaise
1 small red onion, chopped
2 oranges, peeled and chopped
4 flour tortillas
    Vegetable oil for frying
    Lettuce leaves, sliced avocado,
    peeled orange slices, red
    onion rings and BLUE
    DIAMOND® Blanched Slivered
    Almonds for garnish

Cut chicken into 1-inch cubes;
reserve. Sauté almonds in
2 teaspoons oil until golden;
reserve. Combine lime juice, garlic,
cumin, cayenne and salt. Beat in
mayonnaise and remaining ⅓ cup
oil. Add chicken, onion and
reserved almonds. Gently fold in
oranges. Fry tortillas in oil, one at a
time, turning once, until crisp, puffed
and golden; drain and reserve. (A
ladle can be pressed in the center
of the tortilla while frying to form
shell.) To serve, line each tortilla with
lettuce leaves and top with ¼ of
chicken salad. Garnish each serving
with avocado slices, orange slices,
onion rings and almonds.

Makes 4 servings

Chicken Potato Salad Olé

Hearty Chicken and Rice Soup

10 cups chicken broth
 1 medium onion, chopped
 1 cup sliced celery
 1 cup sliced carrots
 ¼ cup snipped parsley
 ½ teaspoon cracked black
     pepper
 ½ teaspoon dried thyme leaves
 1 bay leaf
 1½ cups chicken cubes (about
     ¾ pound)
 2 cups cooked rice
 2 tablespoons lime juice
     Lime slices for garnish

Combine broth, onion, celery, carrots, parsley, pepper, thyme and bay leaf in Dutch oven. Bring to a boil; stir once or twice. Reduce heat; simmer, uncovered, 10 to 15 minutes. Add chicken; simmer, uncovered, 5 to 10 minutes or until chicken is tender. Remove and discard bay leaf. Stir in rice and lime juice just before serving. Garnish with lime slices.   *Makes 8 servings*

Favorite recipe from **USA Rice Council**

Mandarin Chicken Salad

 1 whole chicken breast, halved
 2 cups water
 4 tablespoons KIKKOMAN® Soy
     Sauce, divided
     Boiling water
 ¾ pound fresh bean sprouts
 1 carrot, peeled and shredded
 ½ cup slivered green onions with
     tops
 2 tablespoons minced fresh
     cilantro or parsley
 ¼ cup distilled white vinegar
 2 teaspoons sugar
 ½ cup blanched slivered almonds,
     toasted

Simmer chicken in mixture of 2 cups water and 1 tablespoon soy sauce in covered saucepan 15 minutes or until chicken is tender.

Meanwhile, pour boiling water over bean sprouts. Drain; cool under cold water and drain thoroughly. Remove chicken and cool. (Refrigerate stock for another use, if desired.) Skin and bone chicken; shred meat with fingers into large mixing bowl. Add bean sprouts, carrot, green onions and cilantro. Blend vinegar, sugar and remaining 3 tablespoons soy sauce, stirring until sugar dissolves. Pour over chicken and vegetables; toss to coat all ingredients. Cover and refrigerate 1 hour. Just before serving, add almonds and toss to combine.   *Makes 4 servings*

Cucumber Chicken Salad

 3 tablespoons CROSSE &
     BLACKWELL® Worcestershire
     Sauce
 2 tablespoons cider vinegar
 2 tablespoons vegetable oil
 1 tablespoon sesame oil
 1 teaspoon sugar
 1 teaspoon Dijon-style mustard
 1 teaspoon grated fresh ginger
 2 cups chopped cooked chicken
 1 cup cooked spinach pasta
     (½ cup uncooked)
 1 cucumber, peeled, seeded and
     sliced
 1 red bell pepper, diced
 ¼ cup dry roasted peanuts

In large bowl, combine Worcestershire sauce, vinegar, oils, sugar, mustard and ginger. Add chicken, pasta, cucumber and red pepper; toss lightly to mix well. Top with peanuts.   *Makes 4 servings*

Hearty Chicken and Rice Soup

Paella Salad

Garlic Dressing (recipe follows)
2½ cups water
1 cup uncooked rice
1 teaspoon salt
¼ to ½ teaspoon powdered
   saffron
2 cups cubed cooked chicken
1 cup cooked deveined medium
   shrimp (about 4 ounces)
1 cup diced cooked artichoke
   hearts
½ cup cooked peas
2 tablespoons chopped salami
2 tablespoons thinly sliced green
   onions
2 tablespoons chopped drained
   pimiento
1 tablespoon minced fresh
   parsley
Lettuce or fresh spinach leaves
1 large tomato, seeded and
   cubed

1. Prepare Garlic Dressing.

2. Place water in 1-quart saucepan; heat to boiling. Stir rice, salt and saffron into water. Reduce heat; cover and simmer 20 minutes. Remove from heat; let stand until water is absorbed, about 5 minutes. Refrigerate about 15 minutes.

3. Place rice, chicken, shrimp, artichoke hearts, peas, salami, onions, pimiento and parsley in large bowl; toss well. Pour dressing over salad; toss lightly to coat. Cover and refrigerate 1 hour.

4. Arrange lettuce on large serving platter or 4 serving plates; top with salad mixture. Garnish with cubed tomato. **Makes 4 to 6 servings**

Garlic Dressing

¾ cup olive or vegetable oil
¼ cup white wine vinegar
1 teaspoon salt
½ teaspoon pepper
1 clove garlic, pressed

1. Mix all ingredients in tightly covered jar. (Dressing can be refrigerated up to 2 weeks.)
Makes 1 cup

Chicken Ragout with Chilies, Tortillas and Goat Cheese

1 cup BLUE DIAMOND® Sliced
   Natural Almonds
6 tablespoons vegetable oil,
   divided
6 corn tortillas
4 boneless skinless chicken breast
   halves
1 cup chicken stock or broth
1 onion, chopped
1 red bell pepper, cut into strips
1 can (7 ounces) whole green
   chilies, cut crosswise into
   ¼-inch strips
1½ teaspoons ground cumin
1 cup heavy cream
½ pound goat cheese
1 tablespoon lime juice
½ to 1 teaspoon salt

Sauté almonds in 1 tablespoon of the oil until golden; reserve. Heat 4 tablespoons of the oil and soften tortillas, one at a time, for about 30 seconds. Drain. Cut tortillas into ½-inch strips; reserve. Poach chicken breasts, in covered saucepan, in barely simmering chicken stock, about 10 minutes or until just tender. Reserve chicken stock; slice chicken into strips. In large skillet, sauté onion and bell pepper in the remaining 1 tablespoon oil, until onion is translucent. Add chilies and cumin; sauté 1 minute longer. Stir in reserved stock and cream; simmer 2 to 3 minutes. Add chicken. Stir in goat cheese; *do not boil*. Add lime juice and salt. Fold in tortilla strips and almonds. **Makes 4 servings**

Tucson Chicken Salad

1 (8-ounce) container BORDEN® or
   MEADOW GOLD® Sour Cream
2 teaspoons WYLER'S® or STEERO®
   Chicken-Flavor Instant Bouillon
1 tablespoon REALIME® Lime Juice
   from Concentrate
½ teaspoon ground cumin
   Dash hot pepper sauce
½ pound smoked cooked chicken
   or turkey breast, thinly sliced
½ pound Cheddar cheese, thinly
   sliced
1 medium apple, cored and
   sliced
1 cup sliced celery
½ cup thin strips pared jicama
   Lettuce leaves
½ cup chopped walnuts, toasted

In medium bowl, combine sour
cream, bouillon, ReaLime® brand,
cumin and hot pepper sauce.
Cover; chill 1 hour. Arrange chicken,
cheese, apple, celery and jicama
on lettuce. Top with nuts. Serve with
dressing.* Refrigerate leftovers.

Makes 4 servings

*For thinner dressing, add milk to
desired consistency.

Chicken and Bacon Salad

1 pound boneless skinless
   chicken breasts, cubed
2 teaspoons CHEF PAUL
   PRUDHOMME'S POULTRY
   MAGIC®
2 teaspoons Worcestershire sauce
4 tablespoons olive oil or
   bacon fat
½ cup minced onion
½ cup minced celery
12 ounces bacon, fried crisp,
   drained and crumbled
2 cups chopped purple cabbage
2 cups chopped green cabbage
1 cup chopped iceberg lettuce
1½ cups Green Onion Salad
   Dressing (recipe follows)
4 large romaine or iceberg
   lettuce leaves
8 tomato wedges or cherry
   tomatoes for garnish

Sprinkle chicken breast with Poultry
Magic® and work in well with your
hands, then work in Worcestershire
sauce.

Heat olive oil in large, heavy skillet.
Cook chicken pieces in hot oil,
stirring quickly with wooden spoon.
Brown chicken on all sides, about
3 to 4 minutes. Add onion and
celery; cook 4 minutes. Place in
large bowl; cover and chill.

Add bacon, cabbages, chopped
lettuce and Green Onion Salad
Dressing to chicken. Cover and
chill. Stir before serving. Serve on
lettuce-lined salad plates garnished
with tomatoes.

Makes 4 servings

Green Onion Salad Dressing

1 egg plus 1 egg yolk*
1 cup plus 2 tablespoons
   vegetable oil
   Scant ½ cup chopped green
   onions
1½ tablespoons Creole mustard or
   brown mustard
1 tablespoon white vinegar
½ teaspoon CHEF PAUL
   PRUDHOMME'S VEGETABLE
   MAGIC®

In blender or food processor, blend
egg and egg yolk until frothy, about
2 minutes. With the motor running
add oil until dressing is thick and
creamy. Add remaining ingredients;
blend well. Refrigerate until ready
to use.   *Makes about 1½ cups*

*Use clean, uncracked eggs.

Zucchini Chicken Soup

Prep time: 10 minutes
Cook time: 10 minutes

½ cup chopped onion
½ cup chopped carrot
1 clove garlic, minced
1 tablespoon butter or margarine
1 cup diced cooked chicken
1 can (16 ounces) DEL MONTE®
   Zucchini with Italian-Style
   Tomato Sauce
1 can (14½ ounces) chicken broth

Saute onion, carrot and garlic
in butter, about 5 minutes. Add
remaining ingredients. Heat through
and serve.   *Makes 5 cups*

Brunswick Stew

1 stewing chicken (about
    4½ pounds), cut into serving
    pieces
2 quarts water
1 stalk celery (including leaves),
    cut into 2-inch pieces
1 small onion, quartered
1 small clove garlic, halved
2 teaspoons salt
1 teaspoon whole peppercorns
1 can (16 ounces) tomatoes, cut
    into 1-inch pieces
¼ cup tomato paste
2 medium potatoes, pared and
    cubed
1 onion, thinly sliced
1 teaspoon sugar
½ teaspoon ground pepper
½ teaspoon dried thyme leaves
⅛ teaspoon garlic powder
    Dash hot pepper sauce
1 package (10 ounces) frozen
    lima beans
1 package (10 ounces) frozen
    whole kernel corn

1. Place chicken, giblets and neck in 5-quart Dutch oven; add water. Heat to boiling; skim off foam. Add celery, quartered onion, garlic, salt and peppercorns; heat to boiling. Reduce heat; cover and simmer until thighs are tender, 2½ to 3 hours.

2. Remove chicken pieces from broth; cool slightly. Remove meat from chicken, discarding bones and skin. Cut enough chicken into 1-inch pieces to measure 3 cups. Reserve remaining chicken for another use.

3. Strain broth through fine strainer, discarding vegetables; skim off fat. Return 1 quart of the broth to Dutch oven. Reserve remaining broth for another use. Add tomatoes, tomato paste, potatoes, sliced onion, sugar, ground pepper, thyme, garlic powder and red pepper sauce. Cook until boiling. Reduce heat; cover and simmer 30 minutes.

4. Add beans and corn to stew. Cook until stew boils. Reduce heat; cover and cook 5 minutes. Add chicken pieces and cook 5 minutes longer. Serve hot.

Makes 6 to 8 servings

Fresh Apricot Thai Salad

2 cups sliced fresh California
    apricots
2 cups cubed cooked chicken
1 cup sliced cucumber, peeled
1 cup bean sprouts, rinsed
¼ cup rice vinegar
1 tablespoon chopped fresh
    cilantro
2 teaspoons sugar
¼ cup vegetable oil
½ teaspoon chili oil
    Lettuce leaves
2 tablespoons coarsely chopped
    peanuts
1 lime, cut into wedges

In large bowl, combine apricots, chicken, cucumber and sprouts; refrigerate. In small bowl, beat vinegar, cilantro and sugar until smooth. Drizzle in oils while vigorously whipping with wire whisk. Toss chilled salad with dressing and arrange on individual plates lined with lettuce. Sprinkle with peanuts and garnish with lime wedges.

Makes 4 servings

Note: Rice vinegar and chili oil can be found in the imported (Oriental) section of the supermarket or in specialty food shops.

Favorite recipe from **California Apricot Advisory Board**

Brunswick Stew

Grilled Chicken Salad

¾ pound boneless skinless
    chicken breast
½ teaspoon salt
½ teaspoon ground black pepper
1½ cups diagonally sliced small
    zucchini
3 cups cooked rice, cooled to
    room temperature
1 can (14 ounces) artichoke
    hearts, drained
¾ cup fresh snow peas,
    blanched*
½ medium red pepper, cut into
    1-inch cubes
⅓ cup light Italian salad dressing
1 teaspoon chopped fresh basil
    leaves
    Lettuce leaves

Season chicken with salt and black
pepper. Grill or broil chicken breast.
Add zucchini during last 5 minutes of
grilling or broiling. Cover and chill
chicken and zucchini; cut chicken
into strips. Combine rice, chicken,
zucchini, artichokes, snow peas and
red pepper in large bowl. Blend
dressing and basil in small bowl.
Pour over salad; toss lightly. Serve on
lettuce leaves.   *Makes 4 servings*

*Substitute frozen snow peas,
thawed, for fresh snow peas, if
desired.

Favorite recipe from **USA Rice Council**

Lime-Chutney
Chicken Salad

2 cups cubed cooked chicken
¾ cup fresh cantaloupe balls
½ cup seedless grapes, halved
½ cup sliced celery
¼ cup coarsely chopped walnuts
2 tablespoons sliced green onion
    Lime-Chutney Dressing (recipe
    follows)
4 melon wedges

In large bowl toss together chicken,
cantaloupe, grapes, celery, walnuts
and green onion. Fold in Lime-
Chutney Dressing; cover and chill.
Spoon salad over melon
wedges.   *Makes 4 servings*

Lime-Chutney Dressing

6 tablespoons low-calorie
    mayonnaise
2 tablespoons chopped chutney
1 tablespoon fresh lime juice
½ teaspoon curry powder
½ teaspoon grated lime peel
⅛ teaspoon salt

In small bowl, combine all
ingredients; mix well.
      Makes about ½ cup

Favorite recipe from **Delmarva Poultry
Industries**

Dijon Asparagus
Chicken Salad

1 cup HELLMANN'S® or BEST
    FOODS® Real, Light or
    Cholesterol Free Reduced
    Calorie Mayonnaise
2 tablespoons Dijon-style mustard
2 tablespoons lemon juice
1 teaspoon salt
½ teaspoon freshly ground black
    pepper
6 ounces tricolor twist or spiral
    pasta, cooked, rinsed with
    cold water and drained
1 pound boneless skinless
    chicken breasts, cooked and
    cubed
1 package (10 ounces) frozen
    asparagus spears, thawed
    and cut into 2-inch pieces
1 red bell pepper, cut into 1-inch
    squares

In large bowl combine mayonnaise,
mustard, lemon juice, salt and black
pepper. Stir in pasta, chicken,
asparagus and red pepper. Cover;
chill.   *Makes 6 servings*

Grilled Chicken Salad

Cold Yogurt Soup

1 cup finely chopped cooked
   chicken
1 teaspoon lemon juice
¾ teaspoon minced fresh dill
   or ¼ teaspoon dried
   dill weed
½ teaspoon salt
⅛ teaspoon garlic powder
   Pinch white pepper
2 cups plain yogurt
1 small cucumber, seeded and
   diced
⅓ cup chopped celery
3 tablespoons thinly sliced green
   onions
   Fresh dill sprig, if desired

Place chicken, lemon juice, dill, salt, garlic powder and pepper in small bowl; toss lightly. Cover and refrigerate 30 minutes.

Place yogurt in medium bowl. Stir with fork or whisk until smooth and creamy. Stir chicken mixture, cucumber, celery and onions into yogurt. Pour soup into serving bowls; garnish with fresh dill.

Makes 4 servings

Creamy Cranberry Chicken Salad

6 cups cubed cooked chicken
1½ cups red seedless grapes,
   halved
1½ cups sliced celery
¾ cup sliced almonds
¾ teaspoon curry powder
   Lettuce leaves
2 packages (12 ounces each)
   OCEAN SPRAY® Cran-Fruit™
   Sauce, any flavor
¼ cup vinegar
2 tablespoons sugar
¼ teaspoon cardamom
1 cup vegetable oil

Combine chicken, grapes, celery, almonds and curry powder. Line 6 plates with lettuce. Divide chicken mixture and place on lettuce. Set aside. Combine Cran-Fruit™ Sauce, vinegar, sugar and cardamom in blender or food processor. With motor running, *slowly* add oil, processing until mixture is thick and creamy. Serve dressing on the side in individual ramekins or drizzle over salad. *Makes 6 servings*

Grape Chef-Style Salad

1½ cups California seedless grapes
5 ounces cooked chicken, cubed
3½ ounces Swiss cheese, cut into
   strips
1 cup sliced mushrooms
2 green onions, sliced diagonally
   into thin strips
   Red Wine Vinaigrette (recipe
   follows)
4 cups torn lettuce

Combine grapes, chicken, cheese, mushrooms and green onions; pour Red Wine Vinaigrette over mixture. Marinate, covered, in refrigerator for 1 hour. Drain; reserve Red Wine Vinaigrette. Arrange lettuce in salad bowl, leaving indentation in center. Spoon marinated grape mixture into center. Pass Red Wine Vinaigrette to serve over greens.

Makes 4 servings

Red Wine Vinaigrette

⅓ cup vegetable oil
3 tablespoons red wine vinegar
½ teaspoon crushed oregano
¼ teaspoon salt
⅛ teaspoon ground pepper
   Dash cayenne pepper

Combine all ingredients; mix well.
Makes about ½ cup

Favorite recipe from **California Table Grape Commission**

Chicken Chutney Salad

Prep time: 15 minutes plus refrigerating

¾ cup MIRACLE WHIP® Salad Dressing
¼ cup mango chutney
4 cups cubed cooked chicken
1 cup chopped peeled jicama
1 cup red grape halves
½ cup chopped celery
   Salt and pepper
½ cup coarsely chopped pecans, toasted
4 OSCAR MAYER® Bacon Slices, crisply cooked, crumbled

• Mix salad dressing and chutney until well blended.

• Add all remaining ingredients except pecans and bacon; mix lightly. Season with salt and pepper to taste. Refrigerate.

• Add pecans and bacon just before serving; mix lightly.

Makes 6 servings

Chunky Chicken Noodle Soup with Vegetables

2 envelopes LIPTON® Noodle Soup Mix with Real Chicken Broth
6 cups water
½ small head escarole, torn into pieces (about 2 cups) or 2 cups shredded cabbage
1 large stalk celery, sliced
1 small carrot, sliced
¼ cup frozen peas (optional)
1 small clove garlic, finely chopped
½ teaspoon dried thyme leaves
2 whole cloves
1 bay leaf
2 cups cubed cooked chicken
1 tablespoon finely chopped parsley

In 3-quart microwave-safe casserole, combine noodle soup mix, water, escarole, celery, carrot, peas, garlic, thyme, cloves and bay leaf. Microwave uncovered at HIGH (Full Power), stirring occasionally, 20 minutes or until vegetables are tender. Stir in chicken and parsley and microwave uncovered at HIGH 1 minute or until heated through. Remove whole cloves and bay leaf. Let stand covered 5 minutes.

Makes about 4 servings

Conventional Directions: In large saucepan or stockpot, combine as above. Bring to a boil, then simmer uncovered, stirring occasionally, 15 to 20 minutes or until vegetables are tender. Stir in chicken and parsley and heat through. Remove whole cloves and bay leaf.

Chinese Chicken Salad

½ cup mayonnaise
2 tablespoons CROSSE & BLACKWELL® Worcestershire Sauce
1 tablespoon sherry
1 teaspoon sugar
1½ cups cubed cooked chicken
1 (8-ounce) can sliced water chestnuts, drained
1 cup seedless red grapes
1 (8-ounce) can pineapple chunks, drained
2 carrots, peeled, shredded
3 green onions, sliced

In large bowl, combine mayonnaise, Worcestershire sauce, sherry and sugar. Add chicken, water chestnuts, grapes, pineapple chunks, carrots and green onions; stir to coat with dressing. Cover and refrigerate 30 minutes.

Makes 4 servings

Cobb Salad

4 boneless skinless chicken breast
   halves, cooked, cooled
⅔ cup vegetable oil
⅓ cup HEINZ Distilled White or
   Apple Cider Vinegar
1 clove garlic, minced
2 teaspoons dried dill weed
1½ teaspoons granulated sugar
½ teaspoon salt
¼ teaspoon pepper
8 cups torn salad greens, chilled
1 large tomato, diced
1 medium green bell pepper,
   diced
1 small red onion, chopped
¾ cup crumbled blue cheese
6 slices bacon, cooked,
   crumbled
1 hard-cooked egg, chopped

Shred chicken into bite-size pieces.
For dressing, in jar, combine oil,
vinegar, garlic, dill, sugar, salt and
pepper; cover and shake vigorously.
Pour ½ cup dressing over chicken;
toss well to coat. Toss greens with
remaining dressing. Line each of
4 large individual salad bowls with
greens; mound chicken mixture in
center. Arrange mounds of tomato,
green pepper, onion, cheese,
bacon and egg around chicken.
Makes 4 servings

Cherry Chicken Salad

1 can (16 ounces) pitted tart
   cherries (about 1½ cups)
4 whole boneless skinless chicken
   breasts
3 cups cooked wild rice
1 cup chopped apple
¾ cup chopped walnuts
½ cup chopped celery
½ cup golden raisins
   Cherry Dressing (recipe follows)
   Lettuce leaves

Drain cherries, reserving ½ cup
cherry juice for Cherry Dressing.
Reserve ¼ cup cherries for garnish.
Add water to remaining juice to
make 1½ cups; place in large
saucepan with chicken breasts.
Cook about 15 minutes or until
chicken is tender. Remove chicken
and dice into small pieces.
Combine chicken, cherries, rice,
apple, walnuts, celery and raisins in
large bowl; cover and chill 1 hour.
Add dressing; mix well. Serve on
lettuce-lined platter; garnish with
reserved cherries.
Makes 8 to 10 servings

Cherry Dressing

½ cup cherry juice (reserved
   from above)
½ cup vegetable oil
½ cup grated Parmesan cheese
3 tablespoons sugar
⅛ teaspoon garlic powder
⅛ teaspoon pepper
⅛ teaspoon basil
⅛ teaspoon oregano

Combine all dressing ingredients
and toss over salad.

Favorite recipe from **New York Cherry
Growers Association**

Italian Bean Soup

1 package (10 ounces) frozen
   or 1 can (15½ ounces) Italian
   green beans, drained
4 cups chicken broth
½ cup tomato sauce
½ teaspoon salt
¼ teaspoon garlic salt
¼ teaspoon dried oregano leaves
⅛ teaspoon dried dill weed
⅛ teaspoon pepper
⅓ cup uncooked alphabet or
   soup macaroni
1 cup finely chopped cooked
   chicken

Place beans in 2-quart saucepan;
add broth, tomato sauce, salt, garlic
salt, oregano, dill and pepper. Cook
over high heat until liquid boils; stir in
macaroni. Reduce heat to low;
cover and simmer 10 minutes. Add
chicken; cook 5 minutes longer.
Serve hot.   *Makes 4 to 6 servings*

Cobb Salad

Dairyland Confetti Chicken

CASSEROLE:
1 cup diced carrots
¾ cup chopped onions
½ cup diced celery
¼ cup chicken broth
1 can (10½ ounces) cream of chicken soup
1 cup dairy sour cream
3 cups cubed cooked chicken
½ cup (4 ounces) sliced mushrooms
1 teaspoon Worcestershire sauce
1 teaspoon salt
⅛ teaspoon pepper

CONFETTI TOPPING:
1 cup sifted all-purpose flour
2 teaspoons baking powder
½ teaspoon salt
2 eggs, slightly beaten
½ cup milk
1 tablespoon chopped green bell pepper
1 tablespoon chopped pimiento
1¼ cups (5 ounces) shredded Wisconsin Cheddar cheese, divided

For casserole: In saucepan, combine carrots, onions, celery and chicken broth. Simmer 20 minutes. In 3-quart casserole, mix soup, sour cream, chicken cubes, mushrooms, Worcestershire sauce, salt and pepper. Add simmered vegetables and liquid; mix well.

For confetti topping: In mixing bowl, combine flour, baking powder and salt. Add eggs, milk, green pepper, pimiento and 1 cup of the cheese. Mix just until well blended. Drop tablespoons of topping onto casserole and bake in 350°F oven for 40 to 45 minutes or until golden brown. Sprinkle with remaining ¼ cup cheese and return to oven until melted. Garnish as desired.
Makes 6 to 8 servings

Favorite recipe from **Wisconsin Milk Marketing Board** © **1992**

Quick 'n Easy Country Captain

3 tablespoons minced onion
1 clove garlic, minced
2 teaspoons curry powder
1 tablespoon butter or margarine
1½ cups chicken broth or bouillon
1½ cups UNCLE BEN'S® Rice In An Instant
1½ cups cubed cooked chicken
1 tomato, chopped
¼ cup raisins
⅓ cup salted peanuts (optional)

Cook onion, garlic and curry powder in butter in medium saucepan 2 to 3 minutes. Add broth; bring to a boil. Stir in rice, chicken, tomato and raisins. Cover and remove from heat. Let stand 5 minutes or until all liquid is absorbed. Sprinkle with peanuts, if desired. *Makes 4 servings*

Dairyland Confetti Chicken

Chicken Milano

Prep time: 5 minutes
Cook time: 20 minutes

2 cloves garlic, minced
4 boneless skinless chicken breast
   halves
½ teaspoon basil, crushed
⅛ teaspoon crushed red pepper
   flakes (optional)
   Salt and pepper to taste
1 tablespoon olive oil
1 can (14½ ounces) DEL MONTE®
   Italian Style Stewed
   Tomatoes*
1 can (16 ounces) DEL MONTE® Cut
   Green Italian Beans or Blue
   Lake Cut Green Beans,
   drained
¼ cup whipping cream

Rub garlic over chicken. Sprinkle
with basil and red pepper. Season to
taste with salt and pepper, if desired.
In skillet, brown chicken in oil. Stir
in tomatoes. Cover and simmer
5 minutes. Uncover and cook over
medium heat, 8 to 10 minutes or
until liquid is slightly thickened
and chicken is tender. Stir in green
beans and cream; heat through.
Do not boil.   **Makes 4 servings**

*You may substitute Del Monte®
Original Style Stewed Tomatoes.

Country Skillet Chicken

5 large cloves fresh California
   garlic
1 tablespoon lemon juice
4 large chicken pieces (about
   2 pounds)
2 tablespoons butter
1 tablespoon vegetable oil
1 cup sliced fresh mushrooms
¾ cup dry white wine
1 bay leaf
½ teaspoon salt
1 teaspoon Dijon-style mustard
½ cup chicken broth
1 tablespoon chopped parsley

Peel garlic. Finely mash, or put
through garlic press, 1 clove garlic.
Mix with lemon juice and rub over
chicken pieces. Let stand 10 minutes.
Melt butter with oil in large skillet
over medium-low heat. Add chicken
pieces and sauté 15 minutes, turning
once. Add mushrooms, wine, bay
leaf, salt and remaining 4 cloves
whole garlic. Cover and cook
10 minutes.

Blend mustard with chicken broth.
Pour over chicken and continue
cooking, covered, until chicken is
tender, 10 to 15 minutes. Remove
chicken and whole garlic cloves to
serving platter; keep warm. Discard
bay leaf. Bring pan liquid to boiling
and cook rapidly a few minutes to
reduce and thicken slightly. Pour
over chicken and sprinkle with
parsley. Serve a whole clove of
soft-cooked garlic with each
portion, to mash into the sauce
as chicken is eaten.

Makes 4 servings

Favorite recipe from **The Fresh Garlic
Association**

Chicken Milano

Chicken au Jardin

1 (2½- to 3½-pound) broiler-fryer chicken, cut up
2 tablespoons butter or margarine
1 large onion, coarsely chopped
1 clove garlic, minced
1 can (10½ ounces) chicken broth
1 teaspoon salt
¾ teaspoon TABASCO® Pepper Sauce
½ teaspoon dried thyme leaves
1 cup chopped cooked ham, pork or veal
2 cups sliced carrots
2 cups cut green beans
1 small zucchini, thinly sliced
3 medium tomatoes, peeled and diced
Hot cooked rice or noodles

In large skillet, sauté chicken pieces a few at a time in butter until golden brown; drain and reserve. Cook onion and garlic in pan drippings until golden. Add chicken broth, salt, Tabasco® sauce, thyme, ham and reserved chicken pieces. Cover and simmer 20 minutes. Add vegetables, placing chicken pieces on top. Simmer 15 minutes until vegetables are crisp-tender and chicken is tender. If desired, thicken sauce by stirring in a mixture of 2 tablespoons flour and 2 tablespoons water. Serve with rice or noodles.

Makes 4 to 6 servings

Perfect Chicken and Pork Pie

2 PET-RITZ® Deep-Dish Pie Crust Shells
½ pound pork sausage
¼ cup butter or margarine
⅓ cup all-purpose flour
1 teaspoon celery seeds
½ teaspoon paprika
½ teaspoon poultry seasoning
¼ teaspoon curry powder
¼ teaspoon salt
⅛ teaspoon pepper
1 can (13¾ ounces) ready-to-serve chicken broth
⅔ cup milk
2 cups cubed cooked chicken
1 package (10 ounces) frozen peas, thawed

Invert 1 pie crust onto waxed paper. Let thaw until flat. Preheat oven and cookie sheet to 375°F. Brown sausage in large skillet over medium-high heat; drain sausage on paper towels. Melt butter in same skillet over medium heat. Blend in flour, celery seeds, paprika, poultry seasoning, curry powder, salt and pepper. Gradually stir in broth and milk. Cook until thickened, stirring constantly. Cook 1 minute more. Add chicken, sausage and peas. Pour into pie crust. Cover with flattened crust. Seal edge. Cut slits for steam to escape. Bake on preheated cookie sheet 45 to 50 minutes or until golden brown.

Makes 6 servings

South-of-the-Border Chicken Bake

1 cup dairy sour cream
½ cup Wisconsin Ricotta cheese or creamed cottage cheese
1 package (3 ounces) cream cheese, softened
3 cups coarsely chopped cooked chicken
3 cups cooked rice, cooked in chicken broth
1½ cups (6 ounces) shredded Wisconsin Monterey Jack cheese
1 can (10¾ ounces) cream of chicken soup
1 can (4 ounces) chopped green chilies, drained
2 tomatoes, coarsely chopped
½ cup pitted ripe olives, drained
½ teaspoon salt
⅛ teaspoon garlic powder
1 cup coarsely crushed corn chips

Blend together sour cream, ricotta cheese and cream cheese until smooth. Add remaining ingredients, except corn chips, to cheese mixture. Pour into ungreased shallow 3-quart baking dish. Sprinkle with corn chips. Bake in preheated 350°F oven for 25 to 30 minutes or until heated through.

Makes 8 to 10 servings

Favorite recipe from **Wisconsin Milk Marketing Board** © 1992

Chicken-Broccoli Rice Skillet au Gratin

4 boneless skinless chicken breast halves
1½ teaspoons basil leaves, crushed
¾ teaspoon garlic powder
⅛ teaspoon ground white pepper
1 tablespoon butter or margarine
1½ cups water
1 package (4.5 ounces) COUNTRY INN® Brand Broccoli Rice Au Gratin
Green onion tops, thinly sliced

Sprinkle chicken with basil, garlic and white pepper. Cook chicken in butter in 10-inch skillet over medium heat until lightly browned, about 2 minutes per side. Remove with slotted spatula; reserve. Add water and contents of rice and seasoning packets to skillet. Stir; bring to a boil. Reduce heat; place reserved chicken over rice. Cover and simmer 20 minutes, or until chicken is tender, stirring once. Remove from heat. Let stand covered 5 minutes. Sprinkle with green onions.

Makes 4 servings

Stir-Fry Chicken with Cranberry

2 whole boneless skinless chicken breasts, cut into strips
2 tablespoons vegetable oil
1 medium-size green bell pepper, cut into strips
1 medium-size onion, sliced
2 stalks celery, thinly sliced (about 1¼ cups)
1 package (12 ounces) OCEAN SPRAY® Cran-Fruit™ Sauce, any flavor
¼ cup wine vinegar
3 tablespoons soy sauce
2 teaspoons cornstarch
1 can (8 ounces) water chestnuts, drained
¼ cup cashews
2 tablespoons pimiento, chopped
Hot cooked rice

Have all ingredients chopped and ready to use before starting to cook. Heat skillet on medium-high 2 to 3 minutes. Stir-fry chicken in oil until lightly browned and tender. Remove chicken and set aside. Add green pepper, onion and celery to skillet; stir-fry 2 to 3 minutes until crisp-tender. In a bowl stir together Cran-Fruit™ Sauce, vinegar, soy sauce and cornstarch. Mix well and add to vegetables with chicken, water chestnuts, cashews and pimiento. Reduce heat; cook 2 to 3 minutes until mixture thickens, stirring constantly. Serve with rice.

Makes 4 to 6 servings

Spicy Thai-Style Chicken and Rice

5 boneless skinless chicken breast halves
¼ cup reduced sodium soy sauce
2 teaspoons peanut or vegetable oil
1 cup UNCLE BEN'S® CONVERTED® Brand Rice
1 large clove garlic, minced
2¼ cups chicken broth
2 tablespoons creamy peanut butter
½ teaspoon red pepper flakes *or* ¼ teaspoon cayenne pepper
1½ cups pea pods, cut in half if large
1 tablespoon finely grated fresh ginger
1 small red bell pepper, cut into short, thin strips
2 tablespoons peanut halves (optional)

Combine chicken and soy sauce in shallow bowl; set aside. Heat oil in 10-inch skillet over medium heat. Add rice and garlic; cook and stir 1 minute. Stir in broth, peanut butter and pepper flakes. Bring to a boil, stirring until peanut butter is melted. Place chicken over rice mixture, adding soy sauce to skillet; reduce heat. Cover and simmer 20 minutes or until chicken is tender. Stir in pea pods and ginger; sprinkle with pepper strips. Remove from heat. Let stand covered until all liquid is absorbed, about 5 minutes. Sprinkle with peanuts, if desired.

Makes 5 servings

Orange Chicken Oriental

3 whole boneless skinless chicken breasts, cut into 2-inch strips
½ teaspoon salt
¼ teaspoon ground ginger
2 tablespoons vegetable oil
1 small garlic clove, minced
1 can (8¼ ounces) pineapple chunks, undrained
1 cup Florida orange juice, divided
1 teaspoon instant chicken bouillon granules
2 tablespoons wine vinegar
⅓ cup sliced celery
1 small green bell pepper, cut into ¼-inch strips
1 small onion, sliced
1 small tomato, cut in wedges
3 tablespoons flour
2 tablespoons soy sauce
1 tablespoon sugar
Hot cooked rice

Sprinkle chicken with salt and ginger. Heat oil in large skillet over medium heat; add chicken and garlic and cook 5 minutes. Add liquid from pineapple, ¾ cup of the orange juice, the bouillon and vinegar. Cover; simmer 10 minutes or until chicken is tender.

Add celery, green pepper and onion. Cover; cook 5 minutes longer. Add tomato wedges and pineapple chunks. In small bowl, blend together flour, soy sauce, sugar and remaining ¼ cup orange juice. Add to skillet and cook, stirring constantly, until mixture thickens and comes to a boil; cook 1 minute longer. Serve over rice, if desired.

Makes 4 servings

Favorite Recipe from **Florida Department of Citrus**

Chicken Pot Pie

Preparation time: 45 minutes

1 10¾-ounce can cream of chicken soup
1 cup milk, divided
½ cup chopped onion
1 3-ounce package cream cheese, softened and cut up
¼ cup chopped celery
¼ cup shredded carrot
¼ cup grated Wisconsin Parmesan cheese
3 cups cubed cooked chicken
1 10-ounce package frozen cut broccoli, cooked and drained
1 cup packaged complete buttermilk pancake mix
1 cup (4 ounces) shredded Wisconsin Sharp Cheddar cheese
1 egg, slightly beaten
1 tablespoon vegetable oil
¼ cup sliced almonds

In large saucepan combine soup, ½ cup of the milk, onion, cream cheese, celery, carrot and Parmesan cheese. Cook and stir until mixture is hot and cream cheese is melted. Stir in chicken and broccoli; heat through. Pour into ungreased 2-quart casserole.

For topping, in medium mixing bowl combine pancake mix and Cheddar cheese. In small mixing bowl stir together egg, remaining ½ cup milk and oil. Add to pancake mixture; stir until well combined. Spoon topping over hot chicken mixture. Sprinkle with nuts. Bake in a 375°F oven for 20 to 25 minutes or until topping is golden brown and chicken mixture is bubbly around the edges. *Makes 6 to 8 servings*

Favorite recipe from **Wisconsin Milk Marketing Board** © 1992

Orange Chicken Oriental

Hearty Chicken Bake

3 cups hot mashed potatoes
1 cup (4 ounces) shredded
    Cheddar cheese
1 can (2.8 ounces) DURKEE® French
    Fried Onions
1½ cups (7 ounces) cubed cooked
    chicken
1 package (10 ounces) frozen
    mixed vegetables, thawed
    and drained
1 can (10¾ ounces) condensed
    cream of chicken soup
¼ cup milk
½ teaspoon DURKEE® Ground
    Mustard
¼ teaspoon DURKEE® Garlic
    Powder
¼ teaspoon DURKEE® Ground Black
    Pepper

Preheat oven to 375°F. In medium
bowl, combine mashed potatoes,
½ cup cheese and ½ can French
Fried Onions; mix thoroughly. Spoon
potato mixture into greased 1½-quart
casserole. Using back of spoon,
spread potatoes across bottom
and up sides of dish to form shell.
In large bowl, combine chicken,
mixed vegetables, soup, milk and
seasonings; pour into potato shell.
Bake, uncovered, at 375°F for
30 minutes or until heated through.
Top with remaining cheese and
onions; bake, uncovered, 3 minutes
or until onions are golden brown. Let
stand 5 minutes before serving.

Makes 4 to 6 servings

Chicken Almond Stir-Fry

5 teaspoons soy sauce
3 teaspoons cornstarch, divided
2 whole boneless skinless chicken
    breasts, cut into 2×¼-inch
    strips
1 cup boiling water
1 teaspoon instant chicken
    bouillon granules
½ teaspoon ground ginger
¼ cup CRISCO® Oil, divided
2 cups fresh broccoli flowerettes
    or 1 package (6 ounces)
    frozen Chinese pea pods,
    thawed
1 medium onion, cut into 1-inch
    pieces
1 clove garlic, minced
½ red or green bell pepper, cut
    into 1½×¼-inch strips
¼ to ½ teaspoon dried crushed
    red pepper
½ cup sliced almonds, chopped
    walnuts or peanuts
    Hot cooked rice

1. Combine soy sauce and 1
teaspoon of the cornstarch in
medium bowl. Add chicken; stir
to coat. Refrigerate 30 minutes.

2. Combine water and bouillon
granules in small bowl. Stir
until dissolved. Add remaining
2 teaspoons cornstarch and
ginger; stir.

3. Heat 2 tablespoons of the Crisco®
oil to 365°F in electric skillet or on
medium-high heat in large heavy
skillet. Add broccoli, onion, garlic
and bell pepper. Stir-fry until
crisp-tender. Remove from skillet with
slotted spoon to serving dish.

4. Heat remaining 2 tablespoons
Crisco® oil in same skillet to 365°F or
on medium-high heat. Add chicken
mixture and crushed red pepper.
Stir-fry until chicken is no longer pink.
Return vegetables to skillet. Add
bouillon mixture. Stir until thickened.
Stir in nuts. Serve with rice.

Makes 4 servings

Hearty Chicken Bake

One Skillet Spicy Chicken 'n Rice

¼ cup all-purpose flour
1 teaspoon LAWRY'S® Seasoned Salt
6 to 8 chicken pieces, skinned
2 tablespoons vegetable oil
2 cans (14½ ounces each) whole peeled tomatoes, undrained and cut up
1 package (1.25 ounces) LAWRY'S® Taco Spices & Seasonings
1 cup thinly sliced celery
1 cup long-grain rice
½ cup chopped onion
Chopped parsley

In plastic bag, combine flour and Seasoned Salt. Add chicken; shake to coat well. In large skillet, brown chicken in oil; continue cooking, uncovered, over low heat 15 minutes. Add remaining ingredients except parsley; blend well. Bring to a boil. Reduce heat; cover and simmer 20 minutes or until liquid is absorbed and chicken is cooked through. Garnish with parsley. *Makes 4 to 6 servings*

Ginger Spicy Chicken

2 whole boneless skinless chicken breasts, halved
Salt
2 tablespoons vegetable oil
1 medium-size red bell pepper, cut into 2×¼-inch strips
1 medium-size green bell pepper, cut into 2×¼-inch strips
1 can (8 ounces) pineapple chunks in juice, undrained
½ cup PACE® Picante Sauce
2 tablespoons chopped cilantro or parsley
2 to 3 teaspoons grated fresh ginger *or* ¾ to 1 teaspoon ground ginger

Sprinkle chicken breasts with salt. Heat oil in large skillet over medium heat. Add chicken; cook about 5 minutes on each side or until light brown and tender. Remove chicken; keep warm. Add pepper strips, pineapple with juice, picante sauce, cilantro and ginger to skillet. Cook, stirring frequently, 5 to 7 minutes or until peppers are tender and sauce is thickened. Return chicken to skillet and heat through. *Makes 4 servings*

Brown Rice Chicken Bake

3 cups cooked brown rice
1 package (10 ounces) frozen green peas
2 cups cubed cooked chicken breast
½ cup cholesterol free, reduced calorie mayonnaise
⅓ cup slivered almonds, toasted (optional)
2 teaspoons soy sauce
¼ teaspoon ground black pepper
¼ teaspoon garlic powder
¼ teaspoon dried tarragon leaves
Vegetable cooking spray

Combine rice, peas, chicken, mayonnaise, almonds, soy sauce and seasonings in bowl. Transfer to 3-quart baking dish coated with cooking spray. Cover and bake at 350°F for 15 to 20 minutes.
Makes 6 servings

Favorite recipe from **USA Rice Council**

One Skillet Spicy Chicken 'n Rice

Chicken in French Onion Sauce

1 package (10 ounces) frozen baby carrots, thawed and drained *or* 4 medium carrots, cut into strips (about 2 cups)
2 cups sliced mushrooms
½ cup thinly sliced celery
1 can (2.8 ounces) DURKEE® French Fried Onions
4 boneless skinless chicken breast halves
¾ cup prepared chicken bouillon
½ cup white wine
½ teaspoon DURKEE® Garlic Salt
¼ teaspoon DURKEE® Ground Black Pepper
DURKEE® Paprika

Preheat oven to 375°F. In 8×12-inch baking dish, combine vegetables and ½ *can* French Fried Onions. Arrange chicken breasts on vegetables. In small bowl, combine bouillon, wine, garlic salt and pepper; pour over chicken and vegetables. Sprinkle chicken with paprika. Bake, covered, at 375°F for 35 minutes or until chicken is tender and juices run clear. Baste chicken with wine sauce and top with remaining onions; bake, uncovered, 3 minutes or until onions are golden brown. *Makes 4 servings*

Microwave Directions: In 8×12-inch microwave-safe dish, combine vegetables and ½ *can* onions. Arrange chicken breasts, skinned-side down, along sides of dish. Prepare wine mixture as above, *except* reduce bouillon to ⅓ cup; pour over chicken and vegetables. Cook, covered, on HIGH 6 minutes. Turn chicken breasts over and sprinkle with paprika. Stir vegetables and rotate dish. Cook, covered, 7 to 9 minutes or until chicken is tender and juices run clear. Baste chicken with wine sauce and top with remaining onions; cook, uncovered, 1 minute. Let stand 5 minutes.

Chicken and Zucchini Lasagne

8 lasagne noodles
3 cups (¼-inch-thick) zucchini slices (about 2 medium)
1 tablespoon butter or margarine
1 jar (12 ounces) HEINZ HomeStyle Chicken Gravy
⅔ cup half-and-half or milk
⅓ cup grated Romano or Parmesan cheese
½ teaspoon dried basil leaves, crushed
¼ teaspoon dried thyme leaves, crushed
1½ cups ricotta cheese
1 egg, slightly beaten
3 green onions, sliced
2 tablespoons chopped fresh parsley
2 cups cubed cooked chicken
1 cup shredded mozzarella cheese
¼ cup grated Romano or Parmesan cheese
¼ cup dry bread crumbs
1 tablespoon butter or margarine, melted
Paprika

Cook lasagne noodles following package directions. In large skillet, lightly sauté zucchini in butter. In medium bowl, combine gravy, half-and-half, ⅓ cup Romano cheese, basil and thyme. Combine ricotta cheese, egg, green onions and parsley. Pour ⅓ of gravy mixture into 3-quart oblong baking dish. Arrange 4 lasagne noodles over gravy. Cover noodles with half of *each*: ricotta mixture, zucchini, chicken, mozzarella cheese. Spoon ⅓ of gravy mixture over cheese; repeat layers, ending with remaining gravy mixture. In small bowl, combine ¼ cup Romano cheese, bread crumbs and melted butter; sprinkle over top of baking dish and dust with paprika. Bake in 350°F oven, 45 minutes; let stand 10 minutes before serving.

Makes 6 to 8 servings

Chicken and Rice Paprikash

1 tablespoon paprika, divided
¾ teaspoon salt
¼ teaspoon pepper
6 medium chicken thighs
1 can (14½ or 16 ounces) whole
   tomatoes
1 teaspoon chicken bouillon
   granules
1 small onion, sliced and
   separated into rings
2 cloves garlic, minced
1 cup UNCLE BEN'S® CONVERTED®
   Brand Rice
1 large green bell pepper, cut
   into thin strips
   Light sour cream or plain yogurt

Combine 1½ teaspoons of the paprika, salt and pepper. Rub seasonings onto chicken thighs, coating all surfaces; set aside. Drain tomatoes, reserving juice. Chop tomatoes; set aside. Add enough water to juice to equal 2 cups. Combine tomato liquid, bouillon granules, onion, garlic and remaining 1½ teaspoons paprika in 12-inch skillet. Bring to a boil. Stir in rice and tomatoes. Arrange chicken thighs on top of rice mixture. Cover tightly and simmer 20 minutes. Add green pepper. Remove from heat. Let stand covered until all liquid is absorbed, about 5 minutes. Serve with light sour cream or plain yogurt, if desired.   *Makes 6 servings*

Country-Style Smothered Chicken

2 slices bacon
2½ to 3-pound broiler-fryer chicken,
   cut up
1 can (10¾ ounces) CAMPBELL'S®
   Condensed Cream of
   Mushroom Soup
1 clove garlic, minced
1 teaspoon dried basil leaves,
   crushed
1 medium onion, sliced
   Hot cooked rice

1. In 10-inch skillet over medium heat, cook bacon until crisp. Transfer to paper towels to drain, reserving drippings in pan. Crumble bacon; set aside.

2. Over medium heat, in hot drippings, cook chicken 10 minutes or until browned on all sides. Spoon off fat.

3. Add soup, garlic and basil; stir until smooth. Heat to boiling. Reduce heat to low. Cover; simmer 20 minutes.

4. Add onion. Cover; simmer 15 minutes more or until chicken is tender and juices run clear, stirring occasionally. Sprinkle with crumbled bacon. Serve with rice.
      Makes 6 servings

Caribbean Chicken

¼ cup butter or margarine
2 whole chicken breasts, halved
1 teaspoon salt, divided
½ teaspoon dried tarragon leaves,
   divided
2 tablespoons lime juice
2 tablespoons water
½ teaspoon TABASCO® Pepper
   Sauce
   Hot cooked rice

Heat butter in skillet. Add chicken breasts, skin-side down. Sprinkle with ½ teaspoon salt and ¼ teaspoon tarragon. Cook over medium heat until browned, about 10 minutes. Turn chicken breasts; sprinkle with remaining salt and tarragon; cook until brown, about 10 minutes. Combine lime juice, water and Tabasco® sauce; pour over chicken. Cover and simmer 10 minutes longer or until chicken is tender. Serve with hot cooked rice.

      Makes 4 servings

Chicken & Pasta Sicilian

4 to 6 boneless chicken breast
   halves, lightly seasoned and
   coated with flour and paprika
Vegetable or olive oil
½ (1-pound) package CREAMETTE®
   Spaghetti or Fettuccini,
   cooked and drained
⅓ cup chopped walnuts, toasted
¼ cup margarine or butter, melted
1 (26-ounce) jar CLASSICO®
   Di Sicilia (Ripe Olives &
   Mushrooms) Pasta Sauce,
   heated

In large skillet, cook chicken breasts
in oil until tender and golden on
both sides. Slice crosswise; set aside.
Toss together hot cooked pasta,
walnuts and margarine. To serve,
arrange chicken and pasta on
plate. Spoon hot pasta sauce over
chicken. Garnish with fresh basil, if
desired. Refrigerate leftovers.

Makes 4 to 6 servings

Lemon Honey Chicken

¼ cup CRISCO® Oil
6 tablespoons lemon juice
2 tablespoons honey
1 teaspoon grated lemon peel
   Dash salt and pepper
6 chicken pieces

1. Combine Crisco® oil, lemon juice,
honey, lemon peel, salt and pepper
in glass baking dish. Stir well.

2. Place chicken pieces in baking
dish. Turn to coat. Marinate at room
temperature 20 minutes.

3. Preheat grill.* Remove chicken
from marinade, reserving marinade.

4. Grill chicken 15 to 20 minutes.
Brush with marinade. Grill on other
side 15 to 20 minutes or until meat
near bone is no longer pink.

Makes 4 to 6 servings

*Broiler may also be used.

Chicken & Pasta Sicilian

Magically Moist Chicken

1 (2½- to 3½-pound) broiler-fryer chicken, cut up
½ cup HELLMANN'S® OR BEST FOODS® Real, Light or Cholesterol Free Reduced Calorie Mayonnaise
1¼ cups Italian seasoned bread crumbs

Brush chicken on all sides with mayonnaise. Place bread crumbs in large plastic food bag. Add chicken 1 piece at a time; shake to coat well. Arrange on rack in broiler pan. Bake in 425°F oven about 40 minutes or until golden brown and tender.

Makes 4 servings

Brandied Chicken Thighs with Mushrooms

Prep time: 50 minutes

2½ lbs. (8 to 10) chicken thighs
  Flour
¼ cup PARKAY® Margarine
2 cups mushroom slices
½ cup brandy
1 8-oz. container PHILADELPHIA BRAND® Soft Cream Cheese with Herb & Garlic
  Salt and pepper

• Lightly coat chicken with flour. Brown chicken in margarine in large skillet; remove chicken, reserving liquid in skillet.

• Saute mushrooms in reserved liquid until tender. Stir in brandy. Return chicken to skillet. Cook, covered, 30 minutes or until tender. Place chicken on ovenproof serving platter. Cover; keep warm.

• Skim fat from liquid in skillet; discard fat. Add cream cheese to reserved liquid; stir until mixture is smooth and thoroughly heated. Season with salt and pepper to taste. Pour over chicken.

Makes 4 to 6 servings

Sweet Apricots and Roasted Chicken with Pasta

1 package (10 ounces) bow-tie noodles
1½ cups half-and-half
2 boneless skinless chicken breast halves, roasted and sliced
1 can (17 ounces) California apricot halves, drained and quartered
⅓ cup chopped green onions
2 tablespoons margarine

Cook noodles according to package directions; drain. In a medium saucepan, simmer half-and-half for 4 minutes. Add chicken, apricots, onions and margarine; continue simmering for 2 minutes longer. Season with salt and pepper to taste. Pour over pasta and serve immediately.

Makes 4 servings

Favorite recipe from **California Apricot Advisory Board**

Oriental Chicken

Prep time: 5 minutes
Cooking time: 20 minutes

½ cup MIRACLE WHIP® Salad Dressing
1 tablespoon soy sauce
¼ teaspoon *each* ground ginger and ground red pepper
4 boneless skinless chicken breast halves (about 1¼ pounds)

• Stir together salad dressing, soy sauce and seasonings.

• Place chicken on grill or rack of broiler pan. Brush with half of sauce. Grill or broil 8 to 10 minutes; turn and brush with remaining sauce. Continue grilling or broiling 8 to 10 minutes or until tender.

Makes 4 servings

Variation: For additional flavor, marinate chicken in salad dressing mixture 20 minutes before cooking. Continue as directed.

Baked Chicken Parmesan

Prep time: 15 minutes
Cooking time: 1 hour

1 broiler-fryer chicken, cut up, skinned (2½ to 3 pounds)
¾ cup MIRACLE WHIP® Salad Dressing
1 cup POST TOASTIES® Corn Flake Crumbs
½ cup (2 ounces) KRAFT® 100% Grated Parmesan Cheese
Dash of salt and pepper

• Heat oven to 350°F.

• Brush chicken with salad dressing; coat with combined crumbs and cheese. Sprinkle with salt and pepper.

• Place in 13×9-inch baking dish. Bake 1 hour or until tender.

Makes 3 to 4 servings

Variation: For Cajun Chicken, omit salt. Add 1 teaspoon *each* ground cumin and onion powder and ½ teaspoon *each* ground red pepper and garlic powder to salad dressing; mix well. Substitute 1½ cups crushed sesame crackers for corn flake crumbs and parmesan cheese. Continue as directed.

Note: For crispier chicken, place chicken pieces on rack of broiler pan to bake.

Mexican Chicken Kiev

2 whole boneless skinless chicken breasts (about 1 pound), halved and pounded
4 ounces Monterey Jack cheese, thinly sliced
1 can (4 ounces) chopped green chilies, drained
⅓ cup seasoned dry bread crumbs
1 teaspoon chili powder
½ cup bottled salsa

Preheat oven to 375°F.

Top each chicken breast half with equal amounts of cheese and chilies; roll up and secure with wooden toothpicks. Roll in bread crumbs combined with chili powder, coating well.

In lightly greased shallow baking pan, arrange chicken rolls and bake 20 minutes. Top with salsa and bake an additional 20 minutes or until chicken is tender and no longer pink. Serve, if desired, with additional salsa.

Makes about 4 servings

Microwave Directions: Prepare chicken breasts as above. In lightly greased 2-quart microwave-safe oblong baking dish, arrange chicken. Microwave covered with plastic wrap at HIGH (Full Power) 5 minutes. Rearrange chicken, then top with salsa. Microwave 3 minutes or until chicken is tender and no longer pink. Let stand covered 5 minutes.

Favorite recipe from **Thomas J. Lipton Co.**

Patio Chicken Salad

Prep time: 20 minutes

½ lb. VELVEETA® Pasteurized Process Cheese Spread, cubed
2 cups cubed cooked chicken
1 8-oz. can pineapple chunks, drained
1 cup celery slices
1 cup red or green grape halves
MIRACLE WHIP® Salad Dressing

In large bowl, combine process cheese spread, chicken, pineapple, celery, grapes and enough salad dressing to moisten; mix lightly. Serve on lettuce-covered plates.

Makes 6 servings

Variation: Add ⅓ cup sliced almonds, toasted.

Baked Chicken Parmesan

Chicken Picante

½ cup medium-hot chunky taco
   sauce
¼ cup Dijon-style mustard
2 tablespoons fresh lime juice
3 whole boneless skinless chicken
   breasts, halved
2 tablespoons butter or margarine
   Plain yogurt

Combine taco sauce, mustard
and lime juice in large bowl. Add
chicken, turning to coat. Cover;
marinate in refrigerator at least
30 minutes.

Melt butter in large skillet over
medium heat until foamy. Remove
chicken from marinade; reserve
marinade. Add chicken to skillet;
cook about 10 minutes or until brown
on both sides. Add marinade; cook
about 5 minutes or until chicken
is tender and marinade glazes
chicken. Remove chicken to serving
platter. Boil marinade over high heat
1 minute; pour over chicken. Garnish
with cilantro or lime slices, if desired.
Serve with yogurt.

Makes 6 servings

Favorite recipe from **National Broiler
Council**

Southern Barbecued Chicken

⅔ cup HEINZ Tomato Ketchup
1 tablespoon honey
2 teaspoons lemon juice
   Dash hot pepper sauce
1 (2- to 2½-pound) broiler-fryer
   chicken, cut up

In small bowl, combine ketchup,
honey, lemon juice and hot pepper
sauce. Broil or grill chicken 25 to
30 minutes, turning once. Brush
ketchup mixture on chicken; cook
additional 5 to 10 minutes or until
chicken is tender, turning and
brushing with ketchup mixture.

*Makes 4 to 5 servings
(about ¾ cup sauce)*

Jiffy Chicken 'n Rice

1½ cups cooked unsalted regular
   rice (½ cup uncooked)
1 jar (8 ounces) pasteurized
   processed cheese spread
¼ cup milk
2 cups (10 ounces) cubed cooked
   chicken
1 package (10 ounces) frozen
   peas, thawed and drained
1 can (2.8 ounces) DURKEE® French
   Fried Onions

Preheat oven to 375°F. To hot rice in
saucepan, add cheese spread,
milk, chicken, peas and ½ can
French Fried Onions; stir well. Spoon
into 1½-quart casserole. Bake,
uncovered, at 375°F for 25 minutes
or until heated through. Top with
remaining onions; bake, uncovered,
3 minutes or until onions are golden
brown.   *Makes 4 to 6 servings*

Microwave Directions: Prepare rice
mixture as above; spoon into
1½-quart microwave-safe casserole.
Cook, covered, on HIGH 8 to
10 minutes or until heated through.
Stir rice mixture halfway through
cooking time. Top with remaining
onions; cook, uncovered, 1 minute.
Let stand 5 minutes.

Ortega® Salsa Chicken

4 boneless chicken breast halves
   (about 1 pound)
1 tablespoon vegetable oil
1 (12-ounce) jar ORTEGA® Thick 'n
   Chunky Salsa

In large skillet over medium-high
heat, brown chicken in hot oil; drain
fat. Add salsa and heat to a boil.
Reduce heat to low; cover and
simmer 15 minutes or until chicken is
tender, turning once.

Makes 4 servings

Chicken Picante

Lemon-Broccoli Chicken

1 lemon
1 tablespoon vegetable oil
2 whole chicken breasts, split, skinned and boned (about 1 pound boneless)
1 can (10¾ ounces) CAMPBELL'S® Condensed Cream of Broccoli or Cream of Mushroom Soup
¼ cup milk
⅛ teaspoon pepper

1. Cut 4 thin slices of lemon; set aside. Squeeze 2 teaspoons juice from remaining lemon; set aside.

2. In 10-inch skillet over medium heat, in hot oil, cook chicken 10 minutes or until browned on both sides. Spoon off fat.

3. Meanwhile, in small bowl, combine soup and milk; stir in reserved lemon juice and pepper. Pour over chicken; top each chicken piece with lemon slice.

4. Reduce heat to low. Cover; simmer 5 minutes or until chicken is tender and juices run clear, stirring occasionally.   *Makes 4 servings*

Quick Italian Chicken

Prep & Cook Time: 25 minutes

4 boneless skinless chicken breast halves
2 cans (14½ ounces each) DEL MONTE® Italian Style Stewed Tomatoes
2 tablespoons cornstarch
½ teaspoon oregano or basil, crushed
¼ teaspoon hot pepper sauce (optional)
¼ cup grated Parmesan cheese

Preheat oven to 425°F. Slightly flatten each chicken breast; place in shallow baking dish. Cover with foil; bake 20 minutes or until tender. Remove foil; drain. Combine tomatoes, cornstarch, oregano and pepper sauce in saucepan. Stir to dissolve cornstarch. Cook, stirring constantly, until thickened. Pour sauce over chicken; top with cheese. Return to oven; bake 5 minutes, uncovered, or until heated through. Garnish with chopped parsley and serve with hot cooked rice, if desired.

Makes 4 servings

Variation: Substitute DEL MONTE® Original, Cajun or Mexican Style Stewed Tomatoes for Italian Style.

Chicken and Rice en Croute

1 package refrigerated pizza dough
1 package (12 ounces) OCEAN SPRAY® Cran-Fruit™ Sauce, any flavor
4 boneless chicken breasts, cooked
1 cup prepared long grain and wild rice mix

Preheat oven to 350°F. Lightly grease cookie sheet. Unroll dough and cut in half crosswise, making two 8×8-inch squares. Slightly drain Cran-Fruit™ Sauce.

Place dough on cookie sheet. In center of each square place 2 chicken breasts, ½ cup rice and ½ package of Cran-Fruit™ Sauce. Bring sides of square to center and firmly pinch dough together to seal. Seal ends. Bake for 30 minutes or until golden brown. Cut into pieces to serve.   *Makes 4 servings*

Variation: Substitute 1 cup prepared stuffing in place of rice.

Saucy Chicken Breasts

2 tablespoons CRISCO®
    Shortening
1 package boneless skinless
    chicken breast fillets (about
    1 pound)
2 large green onions with tops,
    chopped (about ½ cup)
1 can (8¼ ounces) sliced, stewed
    tomatoes, undrained
¼ cup dairy sour cream
½ teaspoon dried thyme leaves

1. Melt Crisco® in large, heavy skillet on medium-high heat. Add chicken breasts. Cook 5 minutes per side or until chicken is tender. Remove and set aside.

2. Reduce heat to medium. Add onions and sauté about 3 minutes. Drain off any excess Crisco®.

3. Stir in tomatoes with liquid, sour cream and thyme. Return chicken breasts to pan; spoon sauce over. Cook 5 minutes longer or until heated through. *Do not boil.*

Makes 4 servings

Honey 'n' Spice Chicken Kabobs

1 medium green bell pepper, cut
    into 1-inch squares
4 boneless skinless chicken breast
    halves (about 1 pound)
1 can (8 ounces) pineapple
    chunks, drained
½ cup HEINZ 57 Sauce
¼ cup honey
    Melted butter or margarine

In small saucepan, blanch green pepper in boiling water 1 minute; drain. Cut each chicken breast half into 4 pieces. Alternately thread chicken, green pepper and pineapple onto skewers. In small bowl, combine 57 Sauce and honey. Brush kabobs with butter, then 57 Sauce mixture. Broil, about 6 inches from heat source, 12 to 14 minutes or until chicken is tender, turning and brushing with 57 Sauce mixture once. *Makes 4 servings*

Chicken Broccoli Bake

2 cups chopped cooked broccoli
2 cups cubed cooked chicken
2 cups soft bread cubes
2 cups shredded process sharp
    American cheese
1 jar (12 ounces) HEINZ HomeStyle
    Chicken Gravy
½ cup undiluted evaporated milk

In buttered 9-inch square baking dish, layer broccoli, chicken, bread cubes and cheese. In medium bowl, combine gravy and milk. Season with pepper; pour over chicken-broccoli mixture. Bake in 375°F oven, 40 minutes. Let stand 5 minutes. *Makes 6 servings*

Barbecued Chicken Italiano

½ cup REALEMON® Lemon Juice
    from Concentrate
½ cup vegetable oil
1 teaspoon garlic salt
1 teaspoon oregano leaves
¼ teaspoon pepper
1 (2½- to 3-pound) broiler-fryer
    chicken, cut up

In plastic bag or shallow dish, combine ReaLemon® brand, oil, garlic salt, oregano and pepper; mix well. Add chicken; cover. Marinate in refrigerator 6 hours or overnight, turning occasionally. Remove chicken from marinade; grill or broil as desired, turning and basting frequently with marinade. Refrigerate leftovers.

Makes 4 to 6 servings

Mustard Chicken

**1 (2½- to 3½-pound) broiler-fryer
    chicken, cut up and skinned**
½ cup prepared mustard*
2 tablespoons brown sugar
1 garlic clove, minced
**½ teaspoon dry mustard
    Dry bread crumbs**

Preheat oven to 400°F. Sprinkle chicken pieces with fresh ground pepper.

Combine prepared mustard, brown sugar, garlic and dry mustard; blend well. Spread on both sides of chicken pieces. Dip pieces into bread crumbs, coating lightly. Place on rack in roasting pan and bake until lightly golden, 10 to 15 minutes. *Reduce oven temperature to 350°F.* Continue to bake 20 minutes. Turn pieces over and bake another 30 minutes, or until chicken is tender and coating is crusty.

Makes 4 to 6 servings

*One-quarter cup prepared mustard mixed with ¼ cup Dijon-style mustard can be substituted for the prepared mustard.

Favorite recipe from **The Sugar Association**

Sweet and Spicy Chicken Stir-Fry

Total time: 20 minutes

**1 can (8 ounces) DEL MONTE®
    Pineapple Chunks In Its Own
    Juice**
1 tablespoon vegetable oil
**2 boneless skinless chicken breast
    halves, cut into cubes**
**½ to 1 teaspoon crushed red
    pepper flakes**
**1 can (16 ounces) DEL MONTE®
    Blue Lake Cut Green Beans,
    drained**
¾ cup sweet and sour sauce*

Drain pineapple, reserving ¼ cup juice. In 10-inch skillet, heat oil over medium-high heat. Add chicken; cook 5 minutes, stirring occasionally. Season with salt and pepper, if desired. Stir in reserved juice and red pepper flakes. Reduce heat and cook, uncovered, 2 minutes. Add green beans, pineapple and sauce. Cover and cook 2 minutes or until heated through. Serve over hot cooked rice, if desired.

Makes 4 servings

*Sweet and sour sauce is available in international section of supermarket. Or, combine ½ cup water, ¼ cup sugar, 3 tablespoons apple cider vinegar, 3 tablespoons DEL MONTE® Ketchup and 4 teaspoons cornstarch. Cook, stirring constantly, until thickened and translucent.

Chicken and Wild Rice

**1 package (6 ounces) seasoned
    long grain and wild rice mix**
**1 can (2.8 ounces) DURKEE® French
    Fried Onions**
**4 chicken breast halves or
    2 pounds chicken pieces, fat
    trimmed, skinned if desired**
2⅓ cups water
**½ teaspoon DURKEE® Seasoned
    Salt**
**1 package (10 ounces) frozen
    peas**

Preheat oven to 375°F. In 13×9-inch baking dish, combine uncooked rice and contents of rice seasoning packet; stir in ½ can French Fried Onions. Arrange chicken on rice; pour water over all. Sprinkle chicken with seasoned salt. Bake, covered, at 375°F for 40 minutes. Stir peas into rice. Bake, uncovered, 10 minutes or until chicken and peas are done. Top chicken with remaining onions; bake, uncovered, 3 minutes or until onions are golden brown.

Makes 4 servings

Mustard Chicken

Batter Fried Chicken

1 (2½- to 3½-pound) broiler-fryer chicken, cut up
1 cup water
1 stalk celery (including leaves), cut into 2-inch pieces
1 small onion, cut in half
1 clove garlic, cut in half
½ teaspoon salt
⅛ teaspoon pepper
Fritter Batter (recipe follows)
Vegetable oil for frying

1. Place chicken, water, celery, onion, garlic, salt and pepper in 5-quart Dutch oven. Heat to boiling. Reduce heat to low; cover and cook until chicken is almost tender, 20 to 25 minutes.

2. While chicken is cooking, prepare Fritter Batter. Remove chicken from Dutch oven, drain and pat dry with paper towels. Cool slightly.

3. Pour oil into deep fryer or 5-quart Dutch oven to 2½ to 3 inches deep. Heat to 350°F.

4. Dip chicken in Fritter Batter to coat. Add several chicken pieces to oil. (Do not crowd; pieces should not touch.) Fry, turning occasionally, until chicken is golden, 5 to 7 minutes.

5. Place fried chicken on cookie sheet lined with paper towels; keep warm in 200°F oven until ready to serve. *Makes 4 servings*

Fritter Batter

1 cup all-purpose flour
1 teaspoon baking powder
1 teaspoon salt
¼ teaspoon white pepper
2 eggs
¾ cup milk
1 tablespoon vegetable oil

Combine flour, baking powder, salt and pepper in medium bowl; add eggs, milk and oil. Beat with fork or small whisk until well mixed.
Makes about 1½ cups

Chicken Scandia

1 jar (12 ounces) HEINZ HomeStyle Chicken Gravy
¼ cup dairy sour cream
2 teaspoons lemon juice
1 teaspoon dried dill weed
4 boneless skinless chicken breast halves, grilled or sautéed
Hot cooked noodles

In small saucepan, combine gravy, sour cream, lemon juice and dill; heat over low heat, stirring, until smooth and warm. *Do not boil*. For each serving, slice chicken diagonally across grain into 4 slices. Arrange on a bed of noodles; spoon gravy mixture over chicken. Garnish with lemon wedges, if desired.
Makes 4 servings

Batter Fried Chicken

Zingy Barbecued Chicken

½ cup grapefruit juice
½ cup apple cider vinegar
½ cup vegetable oil
¼ cup chopped onion
1 egg
½ teaspoon celery salt
½ teaspoon ground ginger
⅛ teaspoon pepper
1 (2½- to 3½-pound) broiler-fryer
   chicken, cut up

In blender container, place all ingredients except chicken; blend 30 seconds. In small saucepan, pour blended sauce mixture and heat about 5 minutes, until slightly thickened. Remove from heat; dip chicken in sauce, one piece at a time, turning to thoroughly coat. Reserve sauce.

Place chicken on prepared grill, skin-side up, about 8 inches from heat. Grill, turning every 10 minutes, for about 50 minutes or until chicken is tender and juices run clear. Brush generously with reserved sauce during last 20 minutes of grilling. Watch chicken carefully as egg in sauce may cause chicken to become too brown.

Makes 4 servings

Favorite recipe from **National Broiler Council**

Corn Bread and Sausage Stuffed Chicken

¾ cup chopped BLUE DIAMOND®
   Natural Almonds
1 tablespoon butter
2 hot Italian sausage links
1 small red onion, finely diced
2 cloves garlic, finely chopped
1 small stalk celery, finely diced
3 cups crumbled corn bread
½ cup heavy cream
½ teaspoon salt
¼ teaspoon fresh ground black
   pepper
1 (2½- to 3½-pound) broiler-fryer
   chicken

Sauté almonds in butter until crisp; remove and reserve. Remove casing from sausage and sauté until brown and crumbly. Add onion, garlic and celery; sauté until translucent. Remove from heat. Add corn bread, cream and almonds and mix thoroughly. Season with salt and pepper.

Cut chicken along each side of backbone to remove bone. (Reserve neck, giblets and liver for another use.) With heel of hand, smash the breastbone to flatten. Carefully run hand between meat and skin on both sides of breastbone, loosening skin on breasts, thighs and drumsticks. Stuff corn bread mixture between skin and flesh. Cut a slit in the loose skin on each side of the breastbone end. With drumsticks turned in toward body, insert tips into slits. Bake at 475°F for 10 minutes. *Reduce heat to 350°F* and continue baking 30 minutes or until juice runs clear when thigh is pierced. Let stand 10 minutes before serving.

Makes 4 servings

Note: Chicken roasts more quickly and is easier to carve when its backbone is removed and its breastbone is flattened.

Zingy Barbecued Chicken

Caribbean Pineapple Chicken

Preparation Time: 10 minutes
Cook Time: 20 minutes

1 DOLE® Fresh Pineapple
1 tablespoon vegetable oil
2 boneless skinless chicken breast halves
1 clove garlic, pressed
2 teaspoons all-purpose flour
¼ cup water
2 to 3 tablespoons honey
1 to 2 tablespoons soy sauce
   Grated peel and juice from 1 lime
¼ teaspoon coconut extract
   Pinch ground red pepper
1 tablespoon flaked coconut, optional
1 to 2 teaspoons minced cilantro or green onion, optional

• Twist crown from pineapple. Cut pineapple in half lengthwise. Refrigerate half for another use. Cut fruit from shell with knife. Cut fruit crosswise into 6 slices.

• In 8-inch nonstick skillet, sauté pineapple in oil over medium-high heat until slightly browned. Remove to plates.

• Rub chicken with garlic; sprinkle with flour. In same skillet, sauté chicken, covered, in pan juices over medium-high heat until browned; turn once.

• Mix water, honey, soy sauce, lime juice, coconut extract and red pepper in cup; pour into skillet. Cover; simmer 12 to 15 minutes or until chicken is tender. Remove chicken to serving plates.

• Arrange chicken on plates. Spoon sauce over top. Sprinkle with coconut, lime peel and cilantro.

Makes 2 servings

Delicious Chicken Pasta

2 whole skinless boneless chicken breasts (about 12 ounces)
3 teaspoons CHEF PAUL PRUDHOMME'S MEAT MAGIC®, divided
1 cup chopped onion
½ cup chopped celery
½ cup chopped bell pepper
2 cups defatted chicken stock, divided
2 tablespoons all-purpose flour
3 cups thinly sliced fresh mushrooms
1 teaspoon minced garlic
½ cup chopped green onions
6 ounces pasta (fettucini, angel hair or your favorite), cooked according to package directions

Cut chicken into thin strips; place in small bowl and combine thoroughly with 2 teaspoons of the Meat Magic®.

Place skillet over high heat and add onion, celery, bell pepper and remaining 1 teaspoon Meat Magic®. Cook over high heat, shaking pan and stirring occasionally (don't scrape), for 5 minutes. Add ½ cup chicken stock, scraping up the browned coating on the bottom of pan; cook another 4 minutes. Stir in the chicken mixture and cook 4 minutes. Add flour and stir well, cooking another 2 minutes. Add mushrooms and garlic, folding carefully so mushrooms don't break. Add ½ cup chicken stock and scrape bottom of pan. Cook 4 minutes and add another ½ cup stock, stirring and scraping. Continue cooking 5 minutes more; add green onions and remaining ½ cup stock. Stir and scrape well. Cook 5 more minutes or until chicken is tender; remove from heat. Serve with pasta. *Makes 6 servings*

Caribbean Pineapple Chicken

Chicken Couscous

1½ cups couscous*
2½ cups chicken broth, divided
6 tablespoons butter or
   margarine, divided
1 cup chopped onion
2 tomatoes, peeled and cubed
2 carrots, pared and diagonally
   sliced
1 green bell pepper, cut in strips
½ small butternut squash, pared
   and cubed (2 cups)
1 teaspoon salt
2 cups cubed cooked chicken
1 zucchini, sliced
1 can (20 ounces) chick peas,
   drained
½ cup raisins
1 teaspoon lemon juice
½ teaspoon ground cinnamon
½ teaspoon TABASCO® Pepper
   Sauce
¼ teaspoon ground turmeric
¼ teaspoon paprika
   Hot Sauce (recipe follows)

Place couscous in bowl. Add
1½ cups broth and soak 20 minutes
or until all broth is absorbed. Rub
couscous between fingers to remove
any lumps. Place in colander over
simmering water. Cover; let steam
1 hour. In large saucepan melt
3 tablespoons butter; sauté onion
until tender. Add tomatoes, carrots,
green pepper, butternut squash and
salt. Cover; cook over low heat
30 minutes. Add remaining 1 cup
chicken broth, chicken, zucchini,
chick peas, raisins, lemon juice,
cinnamon, Tabasco® sauce,
turmeric and paprika. Cook
10 minutes longer. Drain off 1 cup
broth to make Hot Sauce. Add
remaining 3 tablespoons butter to
couscous and mix well. Serve
couscous with chicken-vegetable
mixture and Hot Sauce.

Makes 6 servings

*If using quick-cooking couscous,
cook according to package
directions and omit steaming step.

Hot Sauce

1 cup broth drained from chicken-
   vegetable mixture
½ to ¾ teaspoon TABASCO® Pepper
   Sauce
½ teaspoon paprika

Combine all ingredients in small bowl.

California Chicken Risotto

1 pound boneless skinless
   chicken breasts, cut into
   1½-inch pieces
¾ teaspoon salt (optional)
¼ teaspoon ground red pepper
1 tablespoon olive oil
1 large onion, coarsely chopped
   (2 cups)
1 clove garlic, minced
1⅓ cups UNCLE BEN'S® CONVERTED®
   Brand Rice
2 cans (14½ ounces each) ready
   to serve chicken broth
1 small yellow or green bell
   pepper, diced (1 cup)
1 package (3 ounces) cream
   cheese, softened and cut
   into cubes
1 large tomato, chopped
   (1½ cups)
¼ cup fresh basil leaves, thinly
   sliced*

Sprinkle chicken with salt, if desired,
and red pepper; set aside. Heat oil
in 10-inch skillet over medium heat.
Add onion and garlic; cook and stir
3 minutes. Add chicken; cook and
stir until no longer pink. Add rice;
cook and stir 1 minute. Add broth to
skillet; bring to a boil. Reduce heat;
cover tightly and simmer 20 minutes.
Stir in bell pepper. Remove from
heat. Let stand covered until all
liquid is absorbed, about 5 minutes.
Stir in cheese until melted and
creamy. Stir in tomato and basil.

*You may substitute 1 teaspoon
dried basil for fresh; cook with
chicken.

Chicken Tetrazzini

8 ounces uncooked long
    spaghetti, broken in half
3 tablespoons butter, divided
¼ cup all-purpose flour
1 teaspoon salt
½ teaspoon paprika
½ teaspoon celery salt
⅛ teaspoon pepper
2 cups milk
1 cup chicken broth
3 cups chopped cooked chicken
1 can (2 ounces) mushrooms,
    drained
¼ cup pimiento strips
¾ cup grated Wisconsin Parmesan
    cheese, divided

In large saucepan cook spaghetti according to package directions; drain. Add 1 tablespoon of the butter; stir until melted. Set aside. In a 3-quart saucepan melt remaining 2 tablespoons butter; stir in flour, salt, paprika, celery salt and pepper. Remove from heat; gradually stir in milk and chicken broth. Cook over medium heat, stirring constantly, until thickened. Add chicken, mushrooms, pimiento, spaghetti and ¼ cup Parmesan cheese; heat thoroughly. Place chicken mixture on ovenproof platter or shallow casserole; sprinkle remaining ½ cup Parmesan cheese over top. Broil about 3 inches from heat until lightly browned. *Makes 6 to 8 servings*

Favorite recipe from **Wisconsin Milk Marketing Board © 1992**

Double-Coated Chicken

7 cups KELLOGG'S® CORN FLAKES®
    Cereal, crushed to 1¾ cups
1 egg
1 cup skim milk
½ cup all-purpose flour
½ teaspoon salt
¼ teaspoon pepper
3 pounds broiler-fryer chicken
    pieces, washed and
    patted dry
3 tablespoons margarine, melted

1. Measure crushed Kellogg's® Corn Flakes® cereal into shallow dish or pan. Set aside.

2. In small mixing bowl, beat egg and milk slightly. Add flour, salt and pepper. Mix until smooth. Dip chicken in batter. Coat in crumbs. Place in single layer, skin-side up, in foil-lined shallow baking pan. Drizzle with margarine.

3. Bake in preheated 350°F oven about 1 hour or until chicken is tender. Do not cover pan or turn chicken while baking.
Makes 6 servings

Citrus Chicken Iberia

1 (2½- to 3½-pound) broiler-fryer
    chicken, cut into quarters
2 tablespoons all-purpose flour
½ teaspoon salt
⅛ teaspoon pepper
2 tablespoons butter or margarine
2 tablespoons olive oil
1 clove garlic, minced
1 can (6 ounces) Florida frozen
    concentrated orange juice,
    thawed, undiluted
½ cup chicken broth or water
1 teaspoon dried oregano leaves
1 green bell pepper, cut into strips
1 red onion, sliced
½ pound mushrooms, sliced
½ cup black olives, sliced

Wash chicken; pat dry. Combine flour, salt and pepper. Coat chicken with flour mixture. In large skillet, heat butter and oil; sauté garlic until lightly browned. Add chicken and brown on both sides.

Combine orange juice concentrate, chicken broth and oregano; pour over chicken. Cover. Cook for 15 minutes. Baste chicken with pan juices. Add green pepper and onion. Cover; cook 5 minutes longer. Add mushrooms and olives. Cover; cook 5 minutes or until chicken is tender. *Makes 4 servings*

Favorite recipe from **Florida Department of Citrus**

Almond Butter Chicken

4 boneless skinless chicken breast halves (about 1 pound)
2 tablespoons all-purpose flour
½ teaspoon *each* salt and pepper
1 egg, beaten
1 package (2¼ ounces) sliced almonds
¼ cup butter
Orange Sauce (recipe follows)

Place each chicken piece between 2 pieces of plastic wrap. Pound to ¼-inch thickness. Coat chicken with flour. Sprinkle with salt and pepper. Dip 1 side into egg and press into almonds. Melt butter in large skillet. Add chicken, almond-side down. Cook on medium-high heat 3 to 5 minutes or until almonds are toasted; turn. Reduce heat to medium-low and cook 10 to 12 minutes more or until chicken is no longer pink. Serve with Orange Sauce. Garnish as desired.

Makes 4 servings

Orange Sauce

1 tablespoon brown sugar
2 teaspoons cornstarch
Juice from 1 fresh orange (about ½ cup)
2 tablespoons butter
1 teaspoon grated orange peel

Combine sugar and cornstarch in saucepan. Add juice, butter and peel. Cook on medium heat, stirring constantly, until thickened.

Makes ⅔ cup

Favorite recipe from **Wisconsin Milk Marketing Board** © 1992

Classic Chicken Curry with Winter Fruit and Walnuts

4 tablespoons butter
2 cloves garlic, minced
1 tablespoon curry powder
1 teaspoon paprika
¼ teaspoon ground cayenne pepper (optional)
1 tablespoon cornstarch
1 cup chicken broth
6 boneless skinless chicken breast halves
2 pears, cored and thickly sliced
¾ cup chopped California walnuts
½ cup chopped green onions
¼ cup cranberries or currants
Hot cooked rice or couscous (optional)

Microwave butter in uncovered 3-quart glass casserole dish 2 minutes on HIGH. Stir in garlic and spices; microwave on HIGH 3 minutes. Mix cornstarch with broth and add to garlic mixture; stir. Arrange chicken in single layer in sauce. Cover and microwave on HIGH 6 to 8 minutes, stirring every 2 minutes. Stir in pears, walnuts, green onions and cranberries. Cover and cook on HIGH an additional 6 to 8 minutes or until chicken is tender and no longer pink. Arrange chicken and pears on serving platter. Pour remaining sauce over chicken and serve with rice or couscous, if desired.

Makes 4 to 6 servings

Favorite recipe from **California Walnut Marketing Board**

Almond Butter Chicken

Chicken Enchiladas

1 can (10¾ ounces) tomato soup
1 can (10 ounces) enchilada sauce
2 cups plain yogurt, divided
1½ cups finely chopped cooked chicken
1 cup (4 ounces) Wisconsin Mild Cheddar cheese, grated
3 tablespoons vegetable oil
12 small corn tortillas

Preheat oven to 350°F. Combine soup, enchilada sauce and 1 cup of the yogurt until well-blended. Set aside. Combine chicken, cheese and remaining 1 cup yogurt. Heat oil in skillet until hot. Cook tortillas in hot oil, one at a time, just until they become limp. Drain on paper towels. Fill each with 1 heaping tablespoon of chicken mixture and roll up. Arrange rolls, seam-side down, and close together in buttered shallow baking dish. Pour reserved sauce over rolls. Bake 20 to 30 minutes or until thoroughly heated. *Makes 6 servings*

Favorite recipe from **Wisconsin Milk Marketing Board** © 1992

Herb Batter Fried Chicken

1⅓ cups all-purpose flour, divided
1¼ teaspoons salt
1 teaspoon grated lemon peel
1 teaspoon dried marjoram leaves
1 teaspoon sage
1 teaspoon dried thyme leaves
¾ teaspoon paprika
¼ teaspoon pepper
1 egg, slightly beaten
1 cup water
1 (2½- to 3½-pound) broiler-fryer chicken, cut up
CRISCO® Shortening, for frying

1. Combine 1 cup of the flour, the salt, lemon peel, marjoram, sage, thyme, paprika and pepper in medium bowl. Combine egg and water. Add to flour mixture. Stir until well blended.

2. Place remaining ⅓ cup flour in plastic bag. Add chicken, a few pieces at a time. Shake to coat. Dip chicken in batter. Let excess drip off.

3. *To pan fry*: Heat ¼ inch Crisco® to 360°F in electric skillet or on medium-high heat in large heavy skillet. Add chicken; brown. Reduce heat to 275°F for electric skillet or medium-low for skillet. Fry chicken about 30 minutes or until chicken is tender and no longer pink; turn several times. Drain on paper towels.

4. *To deep fry*: Heat 2 or 3 inches Crisco® to 365°F in deep fryer or deep saucepan. Fry chicken, a few pieces at a time, 15 to 20 minutes or until chicken is tender and no longer pink. Drain on paper towels.

Makes 4 servings

Chicken Mexicana

6 boneless skinless chicken breast halves
2 tablespoons vegetable oil
1½ cups chopped onions
⅓ cup sliced scallions
1 package (12 ounces) OCEAN SPRAY® Cran-Fruit™ Sauce, any flavor
½ cup hot salsa
1 cup shredded Monterey Jack cheese with jalapeño peppers

In electric skillet or ovenproof fry pan, cook chicken in hot oil until golden brown on both sides; remove. Add onions and scallions to skillet; cook and stir 1½ to 2 minutes. Stir in Cran-Fruit™ Sauce and salsa; cook until sauce melts. Return chicken breasts to sauce. Reduce heat and cook, covered, about 15 minutes or until chicken is tender, turning chicken over once about halfway through cooking. Sprinkle chicken with cheese. Heat, covered, until cheese melts. Serve with corn bread, if desired.

Makes 6 servings

Herbed Lime Chicken

2 to 3 pounds chicken pieces
½ cup vegetable oil
⅓ cup lime juice
¼ cup chopped onion
2 garlic cloves, minced
1 to 1½ teaspoons TABASCO®
   Pepper Sauce
¾ teaspoon dried rosemary,
   crumbled
½ teaspoon dried marjoram
   leaves, crumbled
½ teaspoon salt

Pierce chicken skin in several places with fork. In shallow dish or plastic bag combine chicken and remaining ingredients. Cover; refrigerate overnight. Drain chicken; reserve marinade. Grill or broil chicken about 20 minutes per side or until chicken is tender and no longer pink. Brush with marinade after turning. Serve with additional Tabasco® sauce, if desired.

Makes 4 servings

Almond Chicken with Onion

1 (2½- to 3½-pound) broiler-fryer
   chicken, cut up
3 tablespoons vegetable oil
2 medium onions, cut in half and
   thinly sliced
3 cloves garlic, finely chopped
2 tablespoons chopped fresh
   cilantro
1 tablespoon chopped fresh
   thyme *or* 1 teaspoon
   dried thyme
½ teaspoon salt
¼ teaspoon freshly grated nutmeg
1 cup chicken stock or broth
⅓ cup amontillado (medium)
   sherry
1 teaspoon lemon juice
¾ cup plus 1 tablespoon BLUE
   DIAMOND® Sliced Natural
   Almonds, toasted and divided

In large skillet, brown chicken in oil. Remove and reserve. Pour off all but 1 tablespoon oil. Add onions and garlic; cook over low heat, stirring, until golden brown. Stir in cilantro, thyme, salt and nutmeg. Add chicken and chicken stock. Cover and cook 15 to 20 minutes or until chicken is tender. Remove chicken and keep warm. Stir in sherry and simmer sauce about 5 minutes or until sauce coats the back of a spoon. Add lemon juice and ¾ cup almonds. Pour sauce over chicken and sprinkle with remaining 1 tablespoon almonds.

Makes 4 servings

Sweet and Spicy Barbecued Chicken

4 tablespoons BUTTER FLAVOR
   CRISCO®, divided
1 (2½- to 3½-pound) broiler-fryer
   chicken, cut up
1 clove garlic, minced
⅓ cup chopped onion
1 can (8 ounces) tomato sauce
¼ cup chili sauce
2 tablespoons honey
1 tablespoon Worcestershire
   sauce
½ teaspoon salt
¼ teaspoon pepper
¼ teaspoon chili powder
¼ teaspoon celery seeds

Preheat oven to 350°F. In large skillet melt 2 tablespoons Butter Flavor Crisco®. Add chicken. Brown over medium-high heat. Place skin-side up in 13×9×2-inch baking pan. Bake at 350°F for 30 minutes.

Meanwhile, in small saucepan melt remaining 2 tablespoons Butter Flavor Crisco®. Add garlic and onion. Cook and stir over medium heat until onion is tender. Stir in tomato sauce, chili sauce, honey, Worcestershire sauce, salt, pepper, chili powder and celery seeds. Remove chicken from oven; drain fat and juices. Pour sauce over chicken. Bake for 35 to 40 minutes longer or until chicken is no longer pink.

Makes 4 to 6 servings

Creole Chicken Thighs

2 tablespoons butter or margarine
½ pound mushrooms, sliced
1 medium onion, chopped
½ cup chopped green bell
   pepper
½ cup thinly sliced celery
2 cloves garlic, minced
1 can (16 ounces) tomatoes,
   cut up
½ teaspoon salt
½ teaspoon sugar
½ teaspoon thyme leaves,
   crumbled
½ teaspoon hot pepper sauce
2 bay leaves
8 broiler-fryer chicken thighs,
   skinned
2 cups cooked rice

In fry pan, melt butter over medium-high heat. Add mushrooms, onion, pepper, celery and garlic. Cook, stirring constantly, about 3 minutes or until onion is translucent but not brown. Stir in tomatoes, salt, sugar, thyme, hot pepper sauce and bay leaves. Add chicken pieces, spooning sauce over chicken. Cook, covered, over medium heat about 35 minutes or until chicken is tender. Remove and discard bay leaves. Serve chicken and sauce over hot cooked rice. *Makes 4 servings*

Favorite recipe from **Delmarva Poultry Industry, Inc.**

Chicken Breasts Hawaiian

4 whole boneless skinless chicken
   breasts, halved
¼ cup butter or margarine
2 teaspoons chili powder
¼ cup flaked coconut
1 egg, slightly beaten
¾ cup coarse dry bread crumbs
1 teaspoon salt
¼ cup plus 2 tablespoons CRISCO®
   Shortening, divided
4 pineapple slices
2 cooked sweet potatoes,
   quartered
2 firm bananas, peeled and cut in
   half lengthwise
   Toasted nuts and coconut,
   if desired
   Sweet and Sour Sauce (recipe
   follows)

1. Rinse and pat chicken dry. Place chicken between 2 pieces of plastic wrap; flatten slightly.

2. Cream butter and chili powder. Blend in coconut. Divide into 8 portions.

3. Spoon 1 portion onto each chicken piece. Tuck in sides; roll and skewer. Chill at least 2 hours.

4. Preheat oven to 400°F.

5. Dip chicken rolls into egg, then roll in combined bread crumbs and salt to coat evenly.

6. Melt ¼ cup of the Crisco® in a large heavy skillet over medium-high heat. Add chicken rolls and brown evenly on all sides. Transfer to greased shallow baking dish and bake 20 to 25 minutes or until chicken is tender. Remove skewers.

7. Melt remaining 2 tablespoons Crisco® in a large heavy skillet over medium heat. Heat pineapple, sweet potatoes and bananas. Arrange with chicken rolls on a serving platter. Garnish with toasted nuts and coconut, if desired. Serve with Sweet and Sour Sauce.
Makes 8 servings

Sweet and Sour Sauce

2 tablespoons CRISCO®
   Shortening
¼ cup finely chopped onion
½ cup catsup
½ cup apricot preserves
1 tablespoon brown sugar
1 tablespoon cider vinegar
½ teaspoon curry powder

1. Melt Crisco® in a small heavy saucepan over medium heat. Add onion; cook until tender. Stir in catsup, apricot preserves, brown sugar, vinegar and curry powder; blend well. Heat and keep warm.

Creole Chicken Thighs

Classic Glorified Chicken

2½ to 3-pound broiler-fryer chicken, cut up
1 tablespoon margarine or butter, melted
1 can (10¾ ounces) CAMPBELL'S® Condensed Cream of Chicken, Cream of Celery, Cream of Mushroom, Golden Mushroom or Cream of Broccoli Soup
Chopped fresh parsley for garnish

1. Preheat oven to 375°F. Meanwhile, in 12×8-inch baking dish, arrange chicken skin-side up. Drizzle with margarine. Bake 40 minutes.

2. Spoon soup over chicken. Bake 20 minutes more or until chicken is tender and juices run clear. Transfer chicken to platter. Stir sauce; spoon sauce over chicken. Garnish with parsley.   *Makes 4 servings*

Mediterranean Chicken

Total time: 30 minutes

½ pound hot Italian sausage links, sliced ¼ inch thick
4 small chicken thighs (about 1 pound)
1 can (14½ ounces) DEL MONTE® Original Style Stewed Tomatoes
1 green pepper, cut into chunks
1 can (17 ounces) DEL MONTE® Whole Kernel Golden Sweet Corn, drained
1 tablespoon cornstarch
1 tablespoon water

In large skillet, lightly brown sausage; push to side. Add chicken; brown. Drain. Stir in tomatoes, pepper and corn; cover and simmer 10 minutes or until chicken is tender. Dissolve cornstarch in water. Stir into chicken mixture. Simmer 5 minutes, stirring occasionally, until heated through.
        Makes 2 to 4 servings

Chicken Cosmopolitan

4 whole boneless chicken breasts
2½ cups hot water
1 teaspoon salt, divided
¼ teaspoon white pepper, divided
2 cups reserved chicken broth*
3 tablespoons butter
3 tablespoons all-purpose flour
1 cup instant nonfat dry milk
1½ teaspoons lemon juice
2 packages (10 ounces each) frozen broccoli spears**
½ cup grated Wisconsin Parmesan cheese
½ cup (2 ounces) Wisconsin Cheddar cheese

Place chicken breasts in heavy saucepan; cover with hot water. Add ½ teaspoon of the salt and ⅛ teaspoon of the pepper; cover and simmer until chicken is tender. Drain off broth; set aside 2 cups for sauce. (If necessary, water may be added to broth to make 2 cups.) Keep chicken hot.

In another saucepan, melt butter; add flour and cook over low heat for 1 minute. Add chicken broth, nonfat dry milk, remaining ½ teaspoon salt and ⅛ teaspoon pepper. Cook, stirring constantly until mixture thickens and is smooth. Remove from heat; stir in lemon juice.

Cook broccoli spears according to package directions until tender; drain and arrange in bottom of large casserole. Place chicken breasts on top of broccoli. Pour sauce over chicken and sprinkle with Parmesan and Cheddar cheeses. Place under broiler for a few minutes to brown. Serve immediately.
        Makes 8 servings

*If cooked chicken is used, 1 can (13¾ ounces) of chicken broth and enough water to make 2 cups may be used for sauce.

**You may substitute asparagus spears for broccoli.

Favorite recipe from **Wisconsin Milk Marketing Board** © **1992**

Chicken Santa Fe

1¾ cups (14½-ounce can)
    CONTADINA® Stewed
    Tomatoes, cut-up
¾ cup chopped onion
¼ cup mild or hot green chili salsa
1 garlic clove, minced
¼ teaspoon salt
4 boneless skinless chicken breast
    halves (about 1 pound)
3 tablespoons all-purpose flour
2 tablespoons olive oil
2 cups hot cooked rice
¼ cup sour cream
1 small ripe avocado, peeled
    and pitted, cut into cubes
    Fresh cilantro or parsley

In medium bowl, combine tomatoes, onion, salsa, garlic and salt; set aside. Coat chicken with flour. In 10-inch skillet heat oil over medium heat. Sauté chicken for 3 to 4 minutes on each side, or until golden brown. Pour tomato mixture over chicken; cover and simmer for 15 to 20 minutes or until chicken is tender. Divide rice onto 4 individual plates. Top with chicken and sauce. Garnish with dollop of sour cream, avocado cubes and cilantro.

Makes 4 servings

Dijon Chicken & Pepper Rice Skillet

1⅔ cups water
2 tablespoons butter or margarine
1 package (5.1 ounces)
    COUNTRY INN® Brand Rice
    Dishes Creamy Chicken &
    Mushroom
2 teaspoons Dijon-style mustard
8 ounces deli-cooked chicken
    breast, cut into ½- to ¾-inch
    cubes
1 cup short thin mixed red and
    green bell pepper strips

Combine water and butter in 10-inch skillet. Stir in contents of rice and seasoning packets and mustard; bring to a boil. Cover tightly; reduce heat and simmer 8 minutes, stirring occasionally. Stir in chicken and pepper strips. Remove from heat; let stand covered 5 minutes or until desired consistency.

Makes 4 servings

Chicken Olé

2 tablespoons vegetable oil
1 large onion, chopped (1 cup)
2 cloves garlic, minced
1 can (10½ ounces) tomato purée
1 cup Florida orange juice
3 tablespoons chopped canned
    green chilies
1 teaspoon grated orange peel
1 teaspoon ground cinnamon
½ teaspoon dried thyme leaves,
    crushed
½ teaspoon salt
1 (2½- to 3½-pound) broiler-fryer
    chicken
    Salt and pepper
8 new potatoes
3 medium-size red bell peppers,
    seeded and sliced

Preheat oven to 350°F. In large skillet, heat oil; sauté onion and garlic until tender. Add tomato purée, orange juice, chilies, orange peel, cinnamon, thyme and salt. Cook 10 minutes, stirring occasionally.

Meanwhile, sprinkle chicken, inside and out, with salt and pepper. Place chicken in large baking dish. Pare a narrow strip around each potato. Arrange potatoes around chicken. Pour sauce over all.

Cover. Bake 45 minutes. Add red peppers; cover. Cook 45 minutes longer until chicken and potatoes are tender. *Makes 4 servings*

Favorite recipe from **Florida Department of Citrus**

Chicken and Broccoli Crepes

½ cup half-and-half
½ cup all-purpose flour
½ teaspoon garlic salt
1¼ cups chicken broth
2 cups (8 ounces) shredded Wisconsin Cheddar cheese, divided
½ cup (2 ounces) shredded Wisconsin Monterey Jack cheese
1½ cups dairy sour cream, divided
2 tablespoons diced pimiento
1 tablespoon dried parsley flakes
1 teaspoon paprika
1 can (4 ounces) sliced mushrooms, drained
2 tablespoons butter
10 cooked Basic Crepes (recipe follows)
2 packages (10 ounces each) frozen broccoli spears, cooked and drained
2 cups cubed cooked chicken

Combine half-and-half, flour and garlic salt; beat until smooth. Blend in chicken broth. Stir in 1 cup of the Cheddar cheese, the Monterey Jack cheese, ½ cup of the sour cream, the pimiento, parsley and paprika. Cook sauce over low to medium heat until mixture thickens, stirring constantly. Sauté mushrooms in butter. On each crepe, place cooked broccoli, chicken and mushrooms. Spoon 1 to 2 tablespoons of sauce over each. Fold crepes. Place in large shallow baking dish. Cover and bake in a preheated 350°F oven 20 to 30 minutes or until throughtly heated. Pour remaining sauce over crepes. Top with remaining 1 cup sour cream and 1 cup Cheddar cheese. Bake, uncovered, 5 to 10 minutes longer or until cheese melts. Top with chopped parsley, if desired.

Makes 10 crepes

Basic Crepes

3 eggs
½ teaspoon salt
2 cups plus 2 tablespoons all-purpose flour
2 cups milk
¼ cup melted butter

Beat eggs and salt. Add flour alternately with milk, beating with electric mixer or whisk until smooth. Stir in melted butter.

Allow crepe batter to stand for 1 hour or more in refrigerator before cooking. The flour may expand and some of the bubbles will collapse. The batter should be the consistency of heavy cream. If the batter is too thick, add 1 to 2 tablespoons of milk and stir well.

Heat 7- to 8-inch nonstick skillet to medium-high heat. Spray lightly with vegetable cooking spray. With one hand pour 3 tablespoons batter and with the other hand lift the pan off heat. Quickly rotate pan until batter covers bottom; return pan to heat. Cook until light brown; turn and brown other side for a few seconds.

Makes about 30 crepes

Note: To store crepes, separate with pieces of waxed paper and wrap airtight. They may be stored frozen for up to 3 months.

Favorite recipe from **Wisconsin Milk Marketing Board © 1992**

Chicken and Broccoli Crepes

Chicken with Cucumbers and Dill

2 whole boneless skinless
    broiler-fryer chicken breasts,
    halved
1 teaspoon salt, divided
¾ teaspoon pepper, divided
4 tablespoons butter or
    margarine, divided
2 cucumbers, peeled, seeded
    and cut into ¼-inch slices
½ teaspoon dill weed
¼ cup lemon juice
    Lemon slices, for garnish

Sprinkle chicken breasts with ½ teaspoon of the salt and ½ teaspoon of the pepper. Melt 2 tablespoons of the butter in large skillet over medium heat; add chicken. Cook about 8 minutes or until chicken is brown on both sides; remove and keep warm. Melt remaining 2 tablespoons butter in same skillet. Add cucumbers; stir to coat. Sprinkle remaining ½ teaspoon salt and ¼ teaspoon pepper over cucumbers; cook 2 minutes. Stir in dill weed. Push cucumbers to side of skillet.

Return chicken and any collected juices to skillet. Cook 2 minutes or until chicken is tender. Place chicken on serving platter; arrange cucumbers around chicken. Cook juices in skillet until light brown. Pour lemon juice and pan juices over chicken. Garnish with lemon slices.

Makes 4 servings

Favorite recipe from **Delmarva Poultry Industry, Inc.**

Chicken Macadamia

6 whole boneless skinless chicken
    breasts
1 cup plus 1 tablespoon
    champagne
4½ teaspoons butter
2½ tablespoons flour
1 cup chicken stock or broth
¼ cup heavy cream
1½ teaspoons chopped fresh
    parsley
    Dash fresh ground pepper
2½ cups Wisconsin Sharp Cheddar
    cheese, shredded
½ cup macadamia nuts, chopped
    and toasted

1. Pound chicken breasts to ¼-inch thickness. Place in large pan and cover with 1 cup champagne. Marinate for 2 hours.

2. Melt butter over low heat. Stir in flour until smooth. Gradually add chicken stock and cream to butter mixture. Cook until smooth and thickened, stirring constantly. Add remaining 1 tablespoon champagne, parsley and pepper. Sauce should be medium thin.

3. Remove chicken from marinade.

4. Combine 2 cups cheese and nuts. Sprinkle ⅓ to ½ cup on each chicken breast. Roll up chicken, tucking in sides; secure with skewers, if necessary. Place seam-side down on baking sheet.

5. Pour half of sauce over chicken breasts; reserve remaining sauce.

6. Bake in 325°F oven for 45 minutes or until chicken is tender.

7. Place chicken breasts on serving plates. Top with remaining ½ cup cheese. Heat remaining sauce; spoon over cheese. Garnish with additional toasted macadamia nuts and chopped parsley, if desired.

Makes 6 servings

Favorite recipe from **Wisconsin Milk Marketing Board © 1992**

Chicken with Cucumbers and Dill

Artichoke-Stuffed Chicken Breasts

2 cups shredded Jarlsberg cheese (8 ounces)
1 teaspoon paprika
½ teaspoon dry mustard
¼ teaspoon dried thyme leaves, crushed
4 whole chicken breasts, split, skinned and boned (about 2 pounds boneless)
1 can (about 14 ounces) artichoke hearts, rinsed, drained and quartered
¼ cup Chablis or other dry white wine
1 tablespoon butter or margarine
1 cup sliced CAMPBELL'S® Fresh Mushrooms
⅛ teaspoon dried thyme leaves, crushed
1 can (10½ ounces) FRANCO-AMERICAN® Chicken Gravy
1 tablespoon chopped fresh parsley

1. In bowl, combine cheese, paprika, mustard and the ¼ teaspoon thyme.

2. Place each chicken breast between sheets of plastic wrap. With meat mallet or rolling pin, pound each chicken breast half to ¼-inch thickness. Divide artichoke quarters among chicken breasts; place *1 tablespoon* of the cheese mixture in center of *each* chicken breast half. Roll up chicken from short end, jelly-roll fashion. Secure with short skewers, if necessary.

3. Place chicken rolls, seam side down, in 12- by 8-inch baking dish. Press remaining cheese mixture on top of each chicken roll. Pour wine into dish. Bake at 350°F for 35 minutes or until chicken is tender and juices run clear. Transfer chicken to platter; keep warm. Reserve ¼ *cup* of the drippings.

4. Meanwhile, in 2-quart saucepan over medium heat, in hot butter, cook mushrooms and the ⅛ teaspoon thyme until mushrooms are tender, stirring often. Add gravy, parsley and reserved drippings; heat through. Serve over chicken rolls.

Makes 8 servings

To Microwave: Prepare chicken rolls as directed in steps 1 and 2, using wooden skewers. Place chicken rolls, seam side down, in 12- by 8-inch microwave-safe baking dish. Pour wine into dish. Cover with waxed paper. Microwave on HIGH 12 minutes or until chicken is tender and juices run clear, rotating twice during cooking. Remove waxed paper. Press remaining cheese mixture on top of each chicken roll. Let stand, uncovered, 5 minutes. Transfer chicken to platter; keep warm. Reserve ¼ *cup* of the drippings; set aside.

In 1-quart microwave-safe casserole, combine butter, mushrooms and the ⅛ teaspoon thyme. Cover with lid; microwave on HIGH 3 minutes or until mushrooms are tender, stirring once during cooking. Stir in gravy, parsley and reserved drippings. Cover; microwave on HIGH 2 minutes or until sauce is hot, stirring once during cooking.

Chicken Parisian

¼ cup unsifted flour
¼ teaspoon paprika
¼ teaspoon pepper
6 boneless skinless chicken breast halves (about 1½ pounds)
3 tablespoons margarine or butter
8 ounces fresh mushrooms, sliced (about 2 cups)
½ cup water
¼ cup dry white wine
2 teaspoons WYLER'S® or STEERO® Chicken-Flavor Instant Bouillon *or* 2 Chicken-Flavor Bouillon Cubes
2 teaspoons chopped parsley
¼ teaspoon dried thyme leaves

In plastic bag, combine flour, paprika and pepper. Add chicken, a few pieces at a time; shake to coat. In skillet, brown chicken in margarine; remove from pan. In same skillet, add remaining ingredients; simmer 3 minutes. Add chicken; simmer, covered, 20 minutes or until tender. Refrigerate leftovers.

Make 6 servings

Chicken Puff Bravo

Prep time: 20 minutes
Cooking time: 40 minutes

- ¾ lb. VELVEETA® Mexican Pasteurized Process Cheese Spread with Jalapeño Pepper, cubed
- ½ cup sour cream
- ¼ teaspoon garlic salt
- 2 eggs, separated
- 2 10-oz. pkgs. BIRDS EYE® Chopped Spinach, thawed, well drained
- 3 cups chopped cooked chicken
- ¼ cup chopped red or green pepper
- 1 4-oz. can sliced mushrooms, drained
- 2 8-oz. cans refrigerated crescent dinner rolls

Preheat oven to 350°F. In 3-quart saucepan, combine process cheese spread, sour cream and garlic salt; stir over low heat until process cheese spread is melted. Remove from heat. Beat egg yolks thoroughly; reserve 1 tablespoon for glaze. Gradually stir remaining egg yolks into cheese mixture. Cool. Beat egg whites until stiff peaks form; fold into cheese mixture. Add remaining ingredients except dough; mix lightly. Unroll one can of dough; press onto bottom and sides of greased 12-inch ovenproof skillet, pressing perforations together to seal. Spread spinach mixture over dough. Unroll second can dough; separate into eight triangles. Loosely twist each triangle at pointed end. Arrange dough triangles on spinach mixture, pointed ends toward the center. Seal outer edges to crust. Brush dough with reserved egg yolk. Bake for 35 to 40 minutes or until egg mixture is set. **Makes 8 servings**

Variation: Substitute 2-oz. jar sliced pimento, drained, for red or green pepper.

Recipe Tip: Substitute 12-inch deep-dish pizza pan for skillet.

Chicken Divan

- 2 packages (10 ounces each) frozen broccoli spears
- ¼ cup CRISCO® Shortening
- ¼ cup all-purpose flour
- ½ teaspoon salt
- 1 cup chicken broth
- ¼ cup crumbled blue cheese
- 1 cup whipping cream
- 3 whole boneless skinless chicken breasts, cooked and sliced
- ¾ cup grated Parmesan cheese, divided

1. Preheat oven to 375°F. Grease 6 broiler-proof* 10-ounce or larger individual baking dishes (ramekins).

2. Cook broccoli in unsalted water in large saucepan just until tender; drain.

3. Melt Crisco® in small saucepan. Blend in flour and salt; cook until mixture bubbles, stirring constantly. Gradually stir in chicken broth. Continue cooking and stirring until sauce comes to a boil and is thickened. Remove from heat. Add blue cheese and stir until melted. Blend in cream with wire whisk.

4. Divide cooked broccoli among ramekins. Spoon about ¼ cup sauce over each serving. Place chicken slices over sauce.

5. Stir half of Parmesan cheese (about 6 tablespoons) into remaining sauce. Spoon equally over chicken. Sprinkle each serving with 1 tablespoon of the remaining Parmesan cheese.

6. Bake at 375°F for 15 minutes or until bubbly and lightly browned. Place broiler rack so that tops of ramekins are about 5 inches from heat source. *Turn temperature control to broil.* Broil 1 to 2 minutes.
Makes 6 servings

*If baking dishes are not broiler-proof, eliminate last broiling step.

Sierra Chicken Bundles

2 cups prepared Mexican or Spanish-style rice mix
¼ cup thinly sliced green onions
½ teaspoon LAWRY'S® Seasoned Pepper
4 whole boneless skinless chicken breasts
½ cup unseasoned dry bread crumbs
¼ cup grated Parmesan cheese
½ teaspoon chili powder
½ teaspoon LAWRY'S® Garlic Salt
¼ teaspoon ground cumin
¼ cup IMPERIAL® Margarine, melted

In medium bowl, combine prepared rice, green onions and Seasoned Pepper. Pound chicken breasts between 2 sheets of waxed paper to ¼-inch thickness. Place about ⅓ cup rice mixture in center of each chicken breast; roll and tuck ends under and secure with wooden skewers. In pie plate, combine remaining ingredients except margarine; blend well. Roll chicken bundles in margarine, then crumb mixture. Place seam-side down in 12×8×2-inch baking dish. Bake, uncovered, in 400°F oven 15 to 20 minutes or until chicken is tender and no longer pink. Remove skewers before serving.   *Makes 4 servings*

Presentation: Serve with assorted steamed vegetables and corn bread.

Almond Chicken Paprika

1 cup BLUE DIAMOND® Whole Natural Almonds, toasted
2 whole boneless skinless chicken breasts, halved
Salt and freshly ground white pepper
8 tablespoons butter, divided
2 teaspoons Dijon-style mustard
2½ tablespoons paprika, divided
Flour
⅔ cup chopped onion
Pinch cayenne pepper
1 cup chicken stock or broth
½ cup sour cream

Coarsely chop almonds; reserve. Lightly flatten chicken breasts. Season with salt and white pepper.

Melt 6 tablespoons of the butter. Whisk in mustard and 1 tablespoon of the paprika. Coat chicken in the flour, then in mustard mixture. Coat with almonds. Place on buttered baking sheet. Bake at 450°F for 10 to 15 minutes or until chicken is just firm. Meanwhile, melt remaining 2 tablespoons butter in saucepan. Add onion and sauté until translucent. Stir in remaining 1½ tablespoons paprika, 1 tablespoon flour, ½ teaspoon salt and cayenne. Cook 1 minute. Stir in chicken stock; simmer 5 minutes. Whisk in sour cream; heat through. *Do not boil.* Divide sauce among 4 serving plates and top each with a chicken breast.

Makes 4 servings

Chicken Americana with Wisconsin Blue Cheese

4 ounces Wisconsin Blue cheese
3 ounces cream cheese, softened
1 egg
2 tablespoons walnuts
3 tablespoons bread crumbs
1 tablespoon chopped parsley
¼ teaspoon pepper
6 whole boneless skinless chicken breasts, pounded
Flour
Butter

Cream cheeses until smooth; combine with egg, walnuts, bread crumbs, parsley and pepper; blend thoroughly. Place ⅓ cup cheese mixture on one side of each chicken breast. Roll to enclose filling; secure with toothpicks.

Flour the rolled chicken breasts lightly. Sauté the breasts in butter until golden brown. (This can be done ahead of time.) Place in baking pan. Bake in a 375°F oven for 20 minutes or until chicken is tender. Remove breasts and let stand 5 to 8 minutes. Slice and serve.

Makes 6 servings

Favorite recipe from **Wisconsin Milk Marketing Board** © 1992

Sierra Chicken Bundles

Herb Marinated Chicken Kabobs

4 boneless skinless chicken breast halves (about 1 pound)
2 small zucchini, cut into ½-inch slices
1 large red bell pepper, cut into 1-inch squares
½ cup HEINZ Gourmet Wine Vinegar
½ cup tomato juice
2 tablespoons vegetable oil
1 tablespoon chopped onion
1 tablespoon brown sugar
2 cloves garlic, minced
½ teaspoon dried oregano leaves
½ teaspoon pepper

Lightly flatten chicken breasts; cut each breast lengthwise into 3 strips. In large bowl, combine chicken, zucchini and red pepper. For marinade, in jar, combine remaining ingredients; cover and shake vigorously. Pour marinade over chicken and vegetables. Cover; marinate in refrigerator about 1 hour. Drain chicken and vegetables, reserving marinade. Alternately thread chicken and vegetables onto skewers; brush with marinade. Broil, 3 to 5 inches from heat source, 8 to 10 minutes or until chicken is cooked, turning and brushing occasionally with marinade. *Makes 4 servings*

Chicken Santiago

4 boneless skinless chicken breast halves
Salt and pepper
⅓ cup chicken broth or water
⅓ cup apple juice
1 tablespoon cornstarch
¼ cup heavy cream
1 cup Chilean seedless red or green grapes, halved
1 green onion, finely sliced
¼ teaspoon dried thyme leaves
⅛ teaspoon ground ginger

Preheat oven to 375°F. Season chicken with salt and pepper. Place in shallow baking dish. Add broth; cover with foil. Bake 20 to 30 minutes, until chicken is tender. Pour ½ cup pan juices into saucepan. Combine apple juice and cornstarch; add to saucepan and stir well. Add remaining ingredients. Cook over medium-high heat until sauce bubbles and thickens, stirring constantly. Season to taste with salt and pepper. Serve sauce over chicken. *Makes 4 servings*

Microwave Directions: Season chicken with salt and pepper. Arrange chicken in round microwaveable dish with thickest ends toward outside of dish. Add broth; cover with waxed paper. Microwave at HIGH (100% power) 6 to 8 minutes or until chicken is tender. Turn and rearrange chicken pieces after 4 minutes. Pour ½ cup pan juices into 2-cup glass measuring cup. Combine apple juice and cornstarch; add to measuring cup and stir well. Add remaining ingredients. Microwave at HIGH (100% power) 4 to 5 minutes or until sauce bubbles and thickens, stirring twice during cooking. Continue as directed.

Favorite recipe from **Chilean Winter Fruit Association**

Coq au Vin

3 to 4 slices bacon, cut into ½-inch pieces
1 (2½- to 3-pound) broiler-fryer chicken, cut up
1 envelope LIPTON® Beefy Mushroom Recipe Soup Mix
½ teaspoon salt
¼ teaspoon dried thyme, crushed
1 clove garlic, minced
1½ cups dry red wine
½ cup water
2 cups frozen small whole onions
2 tablespoons chopped parsley

Cook bacon in large skillet over medium-high heat until crisp. Remove from skillet with slotted spoon; drain on paper towels. Brown chicken in drippings; remove and drain on paper towels.

Stir soup mix, salt, thyme and garlic into drippings in skillet. Then stir in wine and water. Add chicken, bacon, onions and parsley. Bring to a boil over high heat. Reduce heat to low. Cover and simmer 45 minutes or until chicken is tender, basting occasionally.

Makes about 6 servings

Dijon Chicken Elegant

4 whole boneless chicken
    breasts, halved
⅓ cup GREY POUPON® Dijon or
    Country Dijon Mustard
1 teaspoon dried dill weed
    or 1 tablespoon chopped
    fresh dill
4 ounces Swiss cheese slices
2 frozen puff pastry sheets,
    thawed
1 egg white
1 tablespoon cold water

Pound chicken breasts to ½-inch thickness. Blend mustard and dill; spread on chicken breasts. Top each breast with cheese slice; roll up.

Roll each pastry sheet into a 12-inch square; cut each square into 4 (6-inch) squares. Beat egg white and water; brush edges of each square with egg mixture. Place 1 chicken roll diagonally on each square. Join 4 points of pastry over chicken; press to seal seams. Place on ungreased baking sheets. Brush with remaining egg mixture. Bake at 375°F for 30 minutes or until chicken is done. Serve immediately.

Makes 8 servings

Chicken and Vegetable Roll-Ups

1 large carrot, pared and cut into
    thin strips
1 medium red bell pepper,
    seeded and cut into thin strips
1 medium summer squash, cut
    into thin strips
1 medium zucchini, cut into thin
    strips
6 boneless skinless chicken breast
    halves, pounded
2 tablespoons vegetable oil
1 cup plus 2 tablespoons water
1 cup sliced fresh mushrooms
2 teaspoons WYLER'S® or STEERO®
    Chicken-Flavor Instant Bouillon
    or 2 Chicken-Flavor Bouillon
    Cubes
1 tablespoon cornstarch
2 tablespoons dry sherry, optional
½ teaspoon dried tarragon leaves
    Hot cooked rice

Place equal amounts of vegetables on each chicken breast half; roll chicken around vegetables and secure with wooden picks. In large skillet, brown roll-ups in oil. Add *1 cup* water, mushrooms and bouillon; bring to a boil. Reduce heat; cover and simmer 15 minutes. Remove roll-ups from skillet. Combine remaining *2 tablespoons* water and cornstarch. Stir cornstarch mixture, sherry and tarragon into skillet; cook and stir until thickened. Spoon sauce over roll-ups and rice. Refrigerate leftovers.

Makes 6 servings

Champagne Chicken Valencia

½ cup flour
½ teaspoon salt, divided
½ teaspoon pepper, divided
3 whole boneless skinless chicken
    breasts, halved
¼ cup butter
¼ cup vegetable oil
1½ cups dry champagne or white
    wine
1 cup Florida orange juice
1 cup heavy cream
4 Florida Valencia oranges,
    peeled and sectioned*

Preheat oven to 350°F. In small bowl, mix flour with ¼ teaspoon salt and ¼ teaspoon pepper; coat chicken breasts completely with flour mixture.

In large skillet, heat butter and oil; cook chicken until golden brown. Remove from skillet and arrange on greased baking sheet. Bake in 350°F oven 20 minutes or until chicken is tender.

Meanwhile, discard excess fat from skillet. Add champagne, orange juice and remaining ¼ teaspoon salt and ¼ teaspoon pepper; bring to boiling. Add cream and cook over high heat until sauce measures about 2 cups. Place chicken breasts on heated serving platter; top with sauce. Garnish with orange sections.

Makes 6 servings

*When Valencia oranges are not in season, use any in-season orange.

Favorite recipe from **Florida Department of Citrus**

Stuffed Chicken with Apple Glaze

1 (3½- to 4-pound) broiler-fryer
    chicken
½ teaspoon salt
¼ teaspoon pepper
2 tablespoons vegetable oil
1 package (6 ounces)
    chicken-flavored stuffing
    mix, plus ingredients to
    prepare mix
1 cup chopped apple
¼ cup chopped walnuts
¼ cup raisins
¼ cup thinly sliced celery
½ teaspoon grated lemon peel
½ cup apple jelly
1 tablespoon lemon juice
½ teaspoon ground cinnamon

Preheat oven to 350°F. Sprinkle inside of chicken with salt and pepper; rub outside with oil. Prepare stuffing mix according to package directions in large bowl. Add apple, walnuts, raisins, celery and lemon peel; mix thoroughly. Stuff body cavity loosely with stuffing.* Place chicken in baking pan; cover loosely with aluminum foil and roast 1 hour.

Meanwhile, combine jelly, lemon juice and cinnamon in small saucepan. Simmer over low heat 3 minutes or until blended. Remove foil from chicken; brush with jelly mixture. Roast, uncovered, brushing frequently with jelly glaze, 30 minutes longer or until meat thermometer inserted into thickest part of thigh registers 185°F. Let chicken stand 15 minutes before carving. Garnish as desired.   *Makes 4 servings*

*Bake any leftover stuffing in covered casserole alongside chicken until heated through.

Favorite recipe from **Delmarva Poultry Industry, Inc.**

Chicken Provencal with Mushroom Wild Rice

3 whole boneless skinless chicken
    breasts, halved
1 tablespoon olive oil
½ teaspoon salt
¼ teaspoon freshly ground black
    pepper
2 cloves garlic, minced
1 can (14 to 16 ounces) Italian
    plum tomatoes, drained and
    chopped
¼ cup dry red wine
1 tablespoon drained capers
1 teaspoon thyme leaves,
    crushed
2 cups quartered mushrooms
2 tablespoons butter or margarine
2 cups water
1 package (6¼ ounces)
    UNCLE BEN'S® Original Fast
    Cooking Long Grain &
    Wild Rice
½ cup sliced green onions with
    tops

Pound chicken to ½-inch thickness. Cook chicken in oil in 12-inch skillet over medium-high heat until lightly browned, about 1 minute per side. Sprinkle with salt and pepper. Add garlic to skillet; cook 1 minute. Add tomatoes, wine, capers and thyme; stir. Cover and simmer over low heat until chicken is cooked through, about 3 minutes. While chicken simmers, cook mushrooms in butter in medium saucepan over medium-high heat until lightly browned. Add water and contents of rice and seasoning packets to saucepan; bring to a vigorous boil. Reduce heat; cover tightly and simmer until all water is absorbed, about 5 minutes. Remove chicken to serving platter; cook tomato mixture over high heat to desired consistency. Spoon over chicken. Stir green onions into rice; serve with chicken.   *Makes 6 servings*

Stuffed Chicken with Apple Glaze

Gourmet Chicken Bake

1 teaspoon seasoned salt
¼ teaspoon curry powder
¼ teaspoon dried savory, crushed
¼ teaspoon white pepper
3 whole broiler-fryer chicken breasts, halved
1 cup buttermilk or soured milk*
2 packages (6 ounces each) seasoned long grain and wild rice
5½ cups chicken broth, divided
1 pound fresh asparagus, trimmed
2 tablespoons toasted slivered almonds
2 tablespoons chopped pimiento

Combine seasoned salt, curry powder, savory and pepper in small cup. Sprinkle over chicken. Place chicken in large bowl; pour buttermilk over chicken. Refrigerate, covered, overnight. Arrange chicken in single layer in 13×9-inch baking pan. Pour buttermilk marinade over chicken. Bake at 350°F 1 hour or until chicken is tender.

Cook rice according to package directions, using 5 cups of the chicken broth for the water. Meanwhile, cut asparagus 3 inches from tip, then cut remaining stalks into 1-inch pieces. Place asparagus in remaining ½ cup broth in small saucepan. Cover and cook over medium heat 15 minutes. Set aside, but do not drain.

Remove chicken from baking pan. Remove 3-inch asparagus spears from pan; set aside. Stir rice, 1-inch asparagus pieces and broth from asparagus into baking pan. Arrange chicken over rice and place asparagus spears around chicken. Sprinkle with almonds and pimiento. Bake about 15 minutes or until heated through.

Makes 6 servings

*To sour milk, use 1 tablespoon lemon juice or vinegar plus milk to equal 1 cup. Stir; let stand 5 minutes before using.

Favorite recipe from **National Broiler Council**

Breast of Chicken Cordon Bleu

2 whole chicken breasts (about 1 pound each)
Salt and white pepper
½ cup milk
1 egg, slightly beaten
2 slices (1½ ounces each) ham
2 thick slices (2½ ounces each) Medium Wisconsin Aged Swiss cheese
½ cup all-purpose flour
2 cups finely ground dried bread crumbs
½ cup (1 stick) butter

Preheat oven to 350°F. While chicken is ice cold, remove all bones from each whole breast. Do not sever skin at any point. (You may wish to have your butcher do this for you.) Sprinkle both sides of chicken lightly with salt and pepper.

Combine milk and egg to make egg wash. Brush both sides of breasts completely with egg wash. Place each whole breast, skin-side down, on waxed paper. Place one slice of the ham and cheese on half of each breast. Brush ham and cheese liberally with egg wash and fold halves together, wrapping skin around all white meat.

Place flour, remaining egg wash and bread crumbs in 3 separate shallow dishes. Dip rolled chicken in flour, egg wash and crumbs. Be sure crumbs throughly coat chicken. Wrap the coated breasts in foil and refrigerate for 6 hours or overnight.

Remove from refrigerator and brown in butter. Remove from pan; reserve butter. Place chicken in baking pan. Pour reserved butter over chicken. Bake for 35 to 40 minutes or until tender. *Makes 4 servings*

Favorite recipe from **Wisconsin Milk Marketing Board** © **1992**

Gourmet Chicken Bake

Stuffed Chicken Breasts

4 boneless skinless chicken breast
  halves (about 1 pound),
  pounded to ¼-inch thickness
½ teaspoon ground black pepper,
  divided
¼ teaspoon salt
1 cup cooked brown rice
  (cooked in chicken broth)
¼ cup minced tomato
¼ cup (1 ounce) finely shredded
  mozzarella cheese
3 tablespoons toasted rice bran*
  (optional)
1 tablespoon chopped fresh basil
  Vegetable cooking spray

Season insides of chicken breasts
with ¼ teaspoon pepper and salt.
Combine rice, tomato, cheese,
bran, basil and remaining
¼ teaspoon pepper. Spoon rice
mixture on top of pounded chicken
breasts; fold over and secure sides
with wooden toothpicks soaked in
water. Wipe off outsides of chicken
breasts with paper towel. Coat a
large skillet with cooking spray and
place over medium-high heat. Cook
stuffed chicken breasts 1 minute on
each side or just until golden brown.
Transfer chicken to shallow baking
pan. Bake at 350°F for 8 to 10
minutes or until chicken is tender.
Garnish as desired.

Makes 4 servings

*To toast rice bran, spread on
baking sheet and bake at 325°F for
7 to 8 minutes.

Favorite recipe from **USA Rice Council**

Tuscany Chicken and Red Pepper Risotto

6 small boneless skinless chicken
  breasts (about 2 pounds)
1 package (4 to 5 ounces) soft
  herb and garlic cheese
¼ cup finely chopped ripe olives
  or sun dried tomatoes packed
  in oil (optional)
2 tablespoons olive oil, divided
  Salt and pepper
1 cup fresh bread crumbs
  Paprika (optional)
1 large onion, coarsely chopped
2 garlic cloves, minced
1 cup UNCLE BEN'S® CONVERTED®
  Brand Rice
2½ cups chicken broth
1 teaspoon basil leaves, crushed
½ teaspoon salt
½ cup bottled drained roasted red
  peppers or pimientos, cut into
  short thin strips
⅓ cup toasted walnuts

Place chicken breasts on waxed
paper. Combine cheese and olives;
spread over inside of each chicken
breast. Fold over and secure with
wooden picks. Brush chicken lightly
with 1 tablespoon of the oil; sprinkle
with salt and pepper. Roll in bread
crumbs; sprinkle evenly with paprika.
Bake in preheated 400°F oven
30 minutes or until browned and
chicken is tender. While chicken
bakes, heat remaining 1 tablespoon
oil in medium saucepan. Saute
onion and garlic until tender, about
3 minutes. Add rice; cook and stir
1 minute. Add broth, basil and salt;
bring to a boil. Cover tightly and
simmer 20 minutes. Remove from
heat. Let stand, covered, until all
liquid is absorbed, about 5 minutes.
Stir pepper strips and walnuts into
rice; serve with chicken.

Makes 6 servings

Stuffed Chicken Breasts

Chicken Kiev

4 whole boneless skinless chicken
    breasts, halved
1 teaspoon salt
⅓ cup butter or margarine
1 tablespoon minced parsley
1 teaspoon lemon juice
1 clove garlic, minced
1½ cups dry bread crumbs
⅓ cup all-purpose flour
2 eggs, lightly beaten
    CRISCO® Shortening for deep
     frying
    Hot cooked brown rice

1. Sprinkle chicken breasts with salt.

2. Cream butter, parsley, lemon juice and garlic. Spread 2 teaspoons along the center of each chicken breast half. Tuck ends and long sides around flavored butter; skewer or tie to close.

3. Place bread crumbs and flour in separate flat dishes; beat eggs in shallow bowl. Dip each prepared chicken breast first in flour, then eggs and then crumbs. Place seam-side down on plate; refrigerate at least 2 hours or until crumbs are set.

4. Heat 1½-inch layer of Crisco® to 365°F in a deep saucepan or deep fryer. Fry chicken rolls in hot Crisco® for 5 minutes or until tender. Remove with slotted spoon. Serve immediately with brown rice.
Makes 8 servings

Chicken alla Vineyard

4 boneless chicken breast halves
2 tablespoons flour
½ teaspoon basil, finely crushed
½ teaspoon salt
¼ teaspoon tarragon, finely
    crushed
¼ teaspoon paprika
⅛ teaspoon white pepper
1 tablespoon oil
1 tablespoon butter
2 cloves fresh garlic, minced
⅓ cup dry white wine
⅔ cup chicken broth
1 teaspoon lemon juice
1 cup imported winter red grape
    halves, seeded
1 tablespoon finely chopped
    parsley

Remove skin from chicken if desired. Cut chicken breasts in half lengthwise. Combine flour, basil, salt, tarragon, paprika and pepper. Coat chicken; reserve excess flour mixture. Heat oil and butter in skillet. Add chicken and cook over medium-high heat until golden brown on one side. Turn chicken and stir in garlic, reserved seasoned flour mixture and wine. Cover and cook 5 minutes. Add broth, lemon juice and grapes. Cook, uncovered, 5 minutes or just until chicken is tender. Remove chicken and grapes to platter. Boil sauce 1 minute; pour over chicken. Sprinkle with parsley.
Makes 4 servings

Favorite recipe from **Chilean Winter Fruit Association**

Chicken-Asparagus Marsala

2 whole boneless skinless
    broiler-fryer chicken breasts,
    halved
2 tablespoons butter or margarine
1 tablespoon vegetable oil
1 package (10 ounces) frozen
    asparagus spears, partially
    thawed, cut diagonally in
    2-inch pieces
½ pound small mushrooms
¼ cup Marsala wine
¼ cup water
½ teaspoon salt
⅛ teaspoon pepper
1 tablespoon chopped parsley

Pound chicken to ¼-inch thickness. In skillet heat butter and oil. Cook chicken about 5 minutes or until brown, turning once. Remove chicken; set aside. Add asparagus and mushrooms to pan drippings and cook 3 minutes, stirring constantly. Return chicken to pan; add wine, water, salt and pepper. Bring to a boil; boil 2 minutes. Reduce heat; cover and simmer about 3 minutes or until chicken and vegetables are tender. Arrange chicken on platter; spoon vegetable sauce over chicken. Sprinkle with parsley. *Makes 4 servings*

Favorite recipe from **Delmarva Poultry Industry, Inc.**

Acknowledgments

*The publishers wish to thank the following companies
and organizations for the use of their
recipes in this book.*

Best Foods, a Division of CPC International Inc.
Blue Diamond Growers, Inc.
Borden Kitchens, Borden, Inc.
California Apricot Advisory Board
California Table Grape Commission
California Tree Fruit Agreement
California Walnut Marketing Board
Campbell Soup Company
Chef Paul Prudhomme's Magic Seasoning
  Blends™
Chilean Winter Fruit Association
Contadina, Division of Carnation Company
Delmarva Poultry Industry, Inc.
Del Monte Corporation
Dole Food Company
Durkee-French Foods, A Division of Reckitt &
  Colman Inc.
Florida Department of Citrus
The Fresh Garlic Association

Heinz U.S.A.
Kellogg Company
Kikkoman International Inc.
Kraft General Foods, Inc.
Lawry's Foods, Inc.
McIlhenny Company
Nabisco Foods Company
National Broiler Council
Nestlé Specialty Products Company
New York Cherry Growers Association, Inc.
Ocean Spray Cranberries, Inc.
Pace Foods, Inc.
Pet Incorporated
The Procter & Gamble Company, Inc.
The Sugar Association, Inc.
Thomas J. Lipton Co.
Uncle Ben's, Inc.
USA Rice Council
Wisconsin Milk Marketing Board

Photo Credits

*The publishers wish to thank the following companies
and organizations for the use of their
photographs in this book.*

Best Foods, a Division of CPC International Inc.
Delmarva Poultry Industry, Inc.
Del Monte Corporation
Dole Food Company
Durkee-French Foods, A Division of Reckitt & Colman Inc.
Heinz U.S.A.
Kraft General Foods, Inc.
Lawry's Foods, Inc.
National Broiler Council
The Sugar Association, Inc.
USA Rice Council
Wisconsin Milk Marketing Board